I0422999

Limits to Freedom of Association of Civil Society Organizations in Latin America: Comparative view and special case study of Nicaragua, Bolivia, Ecuador, Cuba and Venezuela

Dr. Carlos Eduardo Ponce Silén

Contents

Limitations to Freedom of Association of Civil Society Organizations in Latin America: Comparative view and special case study of Nicaragua, Bolivia, Ecuador, Cuba and Venezuela

"Individuals, groups, institutions and non-governmental organizations have an important role to play and a responsibility in safeguarding democracy, promoting human rights and fundamental freedoms and contributing to the promotion and advancement of democratic societies, institutions and processes."[i]

Summary

Freedom of association is not a matter of good will or special concession from any government; it is a duty. Freedom of association is a fundamental human right embodied in labor movements, freedom of expression, democracy, and among other international instruments ratified by the States. It is an obligation of governments to respect freedom of association and avoid any threats to civil society organizations or activists.

An ongoing backlash against democracy was found in several Latin American countries. Backlash against democracy is the current tendency in several countries that achieved some level of democracy to go backward and dismantle democratic institutions, create their own version of rule of law, limit liberties and attempt against human rights. Traditional and new authoritarian leaders around the world have recently started to crack down on democracy-promotion efforts in their countries. This included direct and more subtle efforts by governments to restrict the right of association and the space of civil society organizations, activists, and interest groups.

I have been developing a study, thanks to the Regan-Fascell Fellowship at the National Endowment for Democracy, which included a view of some trends in authoritarian countries in Latin America against CSOs, current limitations on CSOs or NGOs to operate, international legislation that protects civil society, and some guidelines and recommendations for NGOs and activists to improve their work, even in this restrictive environment. Some of the information for this report came from the excellent research from direct interviews to civil society leaders in the region and the extensive and excellent research from World Movement for Democracy and the International Center for Not-for-Profit Law (ICNL).[1] This study took into account only the "worst" countries in

---

1 The International Center for Not-for-Profit Law ("ICNL") has identified a "growing regulatory backlash against civil society organizations in many parts of the world." ICNL, one of the main organization whose role is defend civil society, notes that, particularly in Latin America, the Middle East, the former Soviet Union and Africa, not-for-profit organizations have encountered a range of obstacles including the outright seizure of assets and facilities, dissolution, de-licensing, restrictions or bans on the use of foreign funding and intimidation.

terms of the number and kinds of restrictions placed against CSOs and other activists; the countries of Alba, or the Bolivarian Alliance of the Americas, a group founded by Venezuela that includes Nicaragua, Bolivia, Cuba, Ecuador, and Venezuela.

Introduction

Freedom of association is not a matter of good will or special concession from any government; it is a duty. Freedom of association is a fundamental human right embodied in labor movements, freedom of expression, democracy, and among other international instruments ratified by the States. It is an obligation of governments to respect freedom of association and avoid any threats to civil society organizations or activists. The *Declaration on Human Rights Defenders*[2] guarantees that everyone has the right to meet peacefully; to form, join, and participate in non-governmental organizations, associations, and groups; and to communicate with non-governmental and intergovernmental bodies, such as the United Nations (UN) and the Organization of American States (OAS). Also, the *Declaration on Human Rights Defenders* specifically provides that everyone is entitled to these rights at the national and international levels, individually, and in association with others.

When analyzing the restrictions against civil society[ii], the first problem is the definition of "civil society". At its most fundamental, civil society is associated with non-government; everything not included in any of the branches of the government. Other groups limited the term to some sectors, like advocacy groups, non-profit organizations, and activists. The problem with all these definitions was how to include business organizations or companies, media conglomerates, unions, and other groups. The more commonly used terms are Non-Governmental Organization (NGO), (which got broader use since its inclusion in the UN Charter, Chapter X, Article 71), civil society organizations or non-profits. In all of these the critical point is the right to freedom of association, or the right of these organizations to operate freely.

Many NGOs, activists, and democracy/human rights defenders find their rights violated by authoritarian or repressive regimes and governments. This is because of their critical roles in promoting human rights awareness, defending the rule of law, promoting democracy principles, defending the environment, promoting environmental justice, educating and empowering citizens, promoting positive changes in terms of policies, and increasing debate on the national and international levels.

Direct actions against groups and individuals include intimidation and harassment, arbitrary arrest and detention, disappearances, torture, and other physical violence. Other forms of repression occur through national legislation, parallel

---

2 Adopted by the United Nations General Assembly on March 8, 1999 (A/RES/53/144)

repressive groups, use of corrupted/controlled judicial systems, and other non-physical activities by governments or followers of a regime.

In several cases national laws and regulations violate the right to freedom of association[iii] by imposing discriminatory restrictions on the right to obtain funding, or require centralized control of international funds by the government entities, impose ridiculous and bureaucratic registration or re-registration procedures, deny access to information, and limit areas of work.

In some countries, like Canada, the government directly or indirectly fosters the existence of an organized "civil society". In others like Zimbabwe, China, or Cuba, the regimes prohibit anything that looks like organized groups. In Latin America, some governments have placed limitations on Civil Society Organizations (CSOs) to operate. The risks of having organized people controlling the public sector, denouncing human rights violations, educating people, or promoting public policy is anathema to authoritarian or quasi-authoritarian regimes.

An ongoing backlash against democracy was found in several Latin American countries. Backlash against democracy is the current tendency in several countries that achieved some level of democracy to go backward and dismantle democratic institutions, create their own version of rule of law, limit liberties and attempt against human rights. Traditional and new authoritarian leaders around the world have recently started to crack down on democracy-promotion efforts in their countries.[3] This included direct and more subtle efforts by governments to restrict the right of association and the space of civil society organizations, activists, and interest groups.[iv] Sometimes, governments have claimed that some restrictions have been necessary to protect sovereignty against foreign aggressors ("the evil empire"), to enhance the accountability of NGOs to fight against extremists, or to coordinate foreign assistance or national security.

Sometimes the situation is more than paradoxical in cases where "civil society" promoted democratic changes. In some countries, as soon as the new government began to rule, the officials began to think about imposing restrictions to CSOs and NGOs.[v]

This research provides a view of some trends in authoritarian countries in Latin America against CSOs, current limitations on CSOs or NGOs to operate, international legislation that protects civil society, and some guidelines and recommendations for NGOs and activists to improve their work, even in this restrictive environment. This study takes into account only the "worst" countries in terms of the number and kinds of

---

3 Thomas Carothers, The Backlash Against Democracy Promotion (Foreign Affairs, March/April, 2006),1 9

restrictions placed against CSOs and other activists; the countries of Alba[4], or the Bolivarian Alliance of the Americas, a group founded by Venezuela that includes Nicaragua, Bolivia, Cuba, Ecuador, and Venezuela. It is an effort to expand the analysis of current backlash against civil society[5] and provide recommendations to civil society organizations. This research will contribute in the following ways to what we know about civil society

   i.   Review current social, political, and ideological environments in Latin America to understand the current backlash in terms of democracy and freedom of association;

  ii.   Summarize current backlash and risk against NGOs in the Alba or Bolivarian Alliance countries, as well as some common patterns in each one of the countries, and similar behaviors against CSOs.

 iii.   Identify the minimum conditions necessary for NGOs to operate freely and effectively in a country by summarizing international human rights instruments that guarantee freedom of association;

 iv.   Document barriers to establishing and nurturing these conditions;

  v.   Summarize best practices or knowledge-at-hand of NGOs to cope with repressive regimes, overcome the barriers they impose, and be effective in their activities.

Sadly for some autocrats, organized civil society groups have been part of the political/social activity for decades and they tend to get stronger when more pressure is applied on them. These groups have been evolving and learning and have become more sophisticated organizations. The globalization of information has helped them to learn from others, from birdwatchers to environmental justice movements, or from civil rights groups to more complex human rights transnational organizations. Civil society goes beyond structures and even with repression, machinations of government intelligence, restrictions to funding, and persecution, the number of organizations, their distribution by areas or geography, size, and membership continues to increase.[vi] But the pressure is still there and the actions from some governments against those groups have been evolving and becoming more sophisticated as well. Repressive and autocratic regimes fear the power of an organized civil society.

This report is organized into three parts.

Part I reviews the backlash against civil society in the Alba countries, common patterns, and similar threats and challenges. The author attempted to find common

---

4 The Bolivarian Alliance for the Peoples of Our America (Alianza Bolivariana para los Pueblos de Nuestra América, or ALBA) is an international agreement directed and organized by the government of Venezuela based on the idea of social, political, and economic integration between countries with similar ideological and political approaches. The countries that are part of the Alba alliance are countries with recent elected pseudo authoritarian-socialist governments or traditional dictatorial countries like Cuba.

5 The International Center for Not-for-Profit Law ("ICNL") has identified a "growing regulatory backlash against civil society organizations in many parts of the world." ICNL, one of the main organization whose role is defend civil society, notes that, particularly in Latin America, the Middle East, the former Soviet Union and Africa, not-for-profit organizations have encountered a range of obstacles including the outright seizure of assets and facilities, dissolution, de-licensing, restrictions or bans on the use of foreign funding and intimidation.

threats against civil society in authoritarian regimes, and similar approaches from those regimes (including some examples of the common threats). This part also includes reviews of regional mechanisms to protect civil society, democracy, and human rights in Latin America and the efficacies of those mechanisms.

Part II provides a comparative view of civil society freedom to operate in the Latin American and Caribbean Region. Some countries have new legislations oriented to regulate civil society organizations in other cases the regulation comes from old civil codes. The report includes a review of all the countries in the Latin American region and a review of the most positive environment to operate for civil society organizations.

Part III of the study will focus its attention to the following questions:

1. How does one develop effective tools to defend civil society in the Americas?
2. How does one improve regional mechanisms to protect civil society organizations?

In this chapter the reader will find practical recommendations based on the common threats and experiences in the region. The goal is to develop a "toolkit" with techniques applied by NGOs in restrictive environments to improve their efficiency and continue their work. This toolkit is a practical contribution to the current backlash in the region. This section also includes some recommendations for improving the Organization of American States' mechanisms to defend civil society and democracy at the regional level, as well as some effective diplomatic tools.

Bias and Methodology

The author is part of what Carruthers (2008) calls academic activism,[6] which consists in the strong tradition of intellectuals and academics who keep one foot in academia and another in the activist community.   He has been a university professor, and human rights and sustainable development activist for more than 20 years. He has taught in several universities and contributed his services in several NGOs, so he has been involved in the social, economic, and political development of Latin American countries as a practitioner.

The methodology implemented in this study was based in part on Cresswell's Elements of Inquiry[7] and it is a mixed mode methodology that includes qualitative and case study data. This study include documental review but some of the information comes from interviews and questionnaires to experts, people that I know that works in Civil Society Organizations with expertise in the field and experts from Civil Society Organizations in Venezuela, Cuba, Ecuador, Nicaragua and Bolivia. I interviewed or received questionnaires[8] of at least 25 experts per country from civil society organizations, media and academia. Due to the risks in their countries and the critical

---

6 David, Carruthers (ed.) Environmental Justice in Latin America: Problems, Promise, and Practice. (MIT Press. Massachusetts, 2008)

7 Cresswell, John (2008)Research Design: Qualitative, Quantitative, and Mixed Methods Approaches, Sage Publications, Inc; 3rd edition

8 Questionnaires included a list of limitations, restrictions or threats and open sections to place cases or personal experiences

information that they provided I cannot use their names in this document or any information suitable to generate any kind of exposure to the sources.

Part I: Freedom of Association, Civil Society and Common Restrictions in Alba Countries

In addition to the behavior of traditional authoritarian regimes in countries such as China, Zimbabwe, Belarus, Cuba, and Burma, new threats have emerged in other countries that have "stable" democracies in Latin America like Venezuela, Bolivia, Nicaragua, and Ecuador. This shift has been called "Backlash" against civil society. Some of these countries introduced restrictive legislation or have implemented measures to restrict the operation of CSOs.

Using the same rhetoric about national security and risk from NGOs controlled by external interests, new legislation and behaviors from Venezuela, Nicaragua, Bolivia, Ecuador, and other countries have similarities in their articles, restrictions, and goals. These similarities among repressive and authoritarian regimes can be compared, for development of a classification system of the barriers and restrictions against civil society.

Two reports, *Defending Civil Society* by the World Movement for Democracy,[9] and *Recent Laws and Legislative Proposals to Restrict Civil Society and Civil Society Organizations* by the International Center for Not-for-Profit Law[10], have described, with examples, some of the restrictions and barriers against NGOs in several countries worldwide. Some of these barriers, with minor modifications, can be seen in several countries. Other studies have also identified other means to limit the rights of association and operation of CSOs.

Common Trends in the Alba Countries

For this paper, some restrictions in the case study countries (Venezuela, Bolivia, Ecuador, Cuba and Nicaragua) were reviewed and compared with trends in international trends and methodologies were developed. Local CSOs from those countries were asked to provide information and examples of each one of the restrictions, limitations, or barriers. These examples were the basis for determining a common pattern of behavior against civil society organizations from authoritarian regimes in the Alba (Bolivarian) countries. The following accounts are the restrictions and some of the examples:

---

9 The World Movement for Democracy is a platform of more than 5800 democracy activists, civil society organizations and democracy groups that joint their efforts to promote democracy practices worldwide.

10 According to their objectives the ICNL is a non-profit organization dedicated to promoting a legal environment in which civil society and public participation can flourish

Barriers to Entry

Limited Rights to Associate and Form NGOs: Some restrictive governments do not grant the right to associate or form organizations. Some examples of this restriction are:

Venezuela Independent CSOs lacks access to registration, notary services, or incorporation. Restriction to participate in government funded projects, since funds are limited to government cooperatives. They also face restriction from participating in projects from IADB, World Bank, etc.

Nicaragua: The government has been denying some organizations from registration due to their "international connections".

Cuba: The Government gives no legal right to association to democracy and human right groups.

Ecuador: NGOs are closely controlled by the government; professional organizations, trade unions, and religious trusts, are subject to particularly substantial government interference. Mandatory licensing is common in Ecuador.[11]

Prohibitions against unregistered groups: Limited registration to certain groups and any activity outside of registration is illegal. Some cases are these

Nicaragua: Any activity from an unregistered group is illegal and can be prosecuted.

Cuba: The government does not allow the registration of CSOs and at the same time forbids any activity of any group, considering it to be illegal. It has been taking activists to jail. There have been several claims of torture against human rights and political activists, persecution, and killings.

Venezuela: Registration is mandatory for any group that wants to operate in Venezuela.

Restrictions on founders: Placing restrictions on eligible founders or requiring difficult-to- reach minimum thresholds for founders is one way to limit the freedom of association. Some examples:

Venezuela: A decision from the Supreme Court (2002) has established that organizations with foreign funding, control, or with integrants from any religious group are illegal. The Law for the Defense of Political Sovereignty and National Self-Determination blocks Venezuelan human rights defenders from receiving international support and severely limits their ability to foster public dialogue with foreign experts who are critical of government policies.

---

11 With the reform of the "Regulation for the Approval of Statutes, Dissolution, Directive Appointment and Registration of the Organizations under Civil Code and Special Laws (CSOs)" (Reglamento para la Aprobación de Estatutos, reformas y codificaciones, liquidación y disolución, y registro de Socios y Directivas, de las organizaciones previstas en el Código Civil y en la Leyes Especiales)(Decreto Ejecutivo No. 982, Registro Civil No. 311 el 8 de abril de 2008) enacted by Presidential Decree No. 982 published in Civil Register No. 311 on April 8, 2008, to incorporate a foundation or non profit or the establishment of any CSO it is mandatory to demonstrate a minimum equity of $ 400 for first-grade corporations (those that bring together individuals with a minimum of five members) and US $ 4,000 for corporations in the second and third degree (which group the first degree and second) and foundations. It also establishes limitations on the nationality of the members and provides broad powers to the government to deny the incorporation.

Bolivia: Only citizens may serve as founders of associations, thereby denying freedom of association to refugees, migrant workers, and stateless persons.

Nicaragua: The activities of the agencies duly registered were deemed inconsistent with the purpose for which they were granted legal status, and violated Article 22 of Act 147 of Associations.

Ecuador: As explained above, the government increasingly confused CSOs (non-profit) with for-profit entities and sought that the list of founders and partners is always available as the virtual records RUOSCs-Single Registration of Civil Society Organizations, and in each ministry where institutions have been approved.[12]

Inability to register and secure the benefits of registration: Registration is necessary for an organization to become, and obtain the rights of, a legal person. Some governments make registration so difficult that some groups are prevented from registering by imposing barriers such as vague registration procedures; detailed, complex documentation requirements; prohibitively high registration fees; and excessive delays in the registration process.[13]

Ecuador: The government has been changing and imposing new requisites for registration and also requesting re-registration and fulfillment of mandatory administrative requirements.[14]

Bolivia: The government has actively discouraged the creation of human rights organizations by simply not responding to registration applications from such groups, sometimes for years.

Venezuela: Even when there is not a limitation for registration, Public Registries tend to reject registration from organizations with human rights or democratic objectives.

---

12 This is a rule for all CSOs that have been approved in the country. This provides a broad tool for the government to increase restrictions on the type of founders and members of the CSOs.

13 In a report, developed by the World Movement for Democracy Steering Committee and the International Center for Not for Profit Law (ICNL) called "Defending Civil Society" we had the opportunity to open consultations for all the regions with meetings in several cities and we found troublesome similarities among different regimes that persecute or imposed limitations/restrictions to civil society. That report came after an intensive consultation process worldwide. According with the report, legal constrains against civil society fall broadly into five categories:

- Barriers to entry (limited right to associate, prohibition against unregistered groups, restrictions on founders, burdensome registration/incorporation procedures, vague grounds for denial, re-registration requirements, barriers for international organizations).
- Barriers for operational Activity (direct prohibitions against spheres of activity, invasive supervisory oversight, government harassment, criminal sanctions against individuals, failure to protect individuals, termination and dissolution, establishment of GONGOs).
- Barriers to Speech and Advocacy (prior restrains and censorship, defamation laws, vague restrictions against advocacy, criminalization of dissent, restrictions on freedom of assembly).
- Barriers to contact and Communication (barriers to the creation of networks, barriers to international contact, barriers to communication, criminal sanctions against individuals).
- Barriers to resources (Prohibition against funding, advance government approval, routing founding through the government).Barriers to contact and Communication (barriers to the creation of networks, barriers to international contact, barriers to communication, criminal sanctions against individuals).
- Barriers to resources (Prohibition against funding, advance government approval, routing founding through the government).

14 The cost and administrative bureaucracy to incorporate or register a group are the most difficult barriers. It is almost impossible to overcome the mandatory administrative procedures, or the tremendous power in the government in terms of the causes of dissolution, which can be as discretionary as non-compliance with the registration or demonstration of enough money.

Nicaragua: Several laws and regulations have been implemented to make it impossible to obtain new registrations or renewals for CSOs.

Denial of registration: A common legal tool is the use of overly broad, vague grounds for denying registration applications; often no appeal mechanism is available.[15] Some examples are: following.

Bolivia: Registration can be refused if "society does not need its services or if there are other associations that fulfill society's needs in the [same] field of activity."

Nicaragua: If an organization allegedly "conspires" against the regime, or a political party doesn't fulfill some vague requirements, they can denied or suspend from registration.

Venezuela: There have been several cases of denials of registrations to organizations that work in democracy or human rights or any activity that can be perceived as opposition to the current regime. Sometimes the registrar's office delays the registration/incorporation for years or simply uses any excuse to not register a group.

Ecuador: Registration may be denied according to the opinion of the government. The Government can deny the application for approval of the CSO if it did not meet the content requirements of the statutes referred to in Article 6 of the Regulation, or not completing the documents established there, or not fulfilling any of the new arbitrary requirements.

Cuba: The state controls any registration of any group and it doesn't allow any registration of CSOs.

Re-registration requirements: Such requirements place a burden on civil society and provide the government with regular opportunities to deny registration.[16]

Ecuador: Laws require renovations and re-registration processes. By Executive Decree No. 177, published in the Official Gazette No. 94, December 23, 2009, CSOs were given 180 days to reform their statutes for the purpose of satisfying the requirements of the Regulation amended by Executive Order 982. Not to comply would be grounds for dissolution. CSOs in Ecuador believe that this is essentially an unconstitutional rule.

Venezuela: The pending Cooperation Law includes a requirement of re-registration to all the NGOs

Barriers for international organizations: Some countries use legal barriers specifically to target international organizations, seeking to prevent or impede their operation inside the country.[17]

Bolivia: International organizations may set up offices, subject to any conditions and restrictions which the Minister imposes. By Presidential Decree the government established the requirement of previous approval from the Ministry of Planning and

---

15 "Defending Civil Society" supra note 6

16 "Defending Civil Society" supra note 6

17 "Defending Civil Society" supra note 6

Development to allow any foreign organization to operate in Bolivia. The government also signed an agreement with the US government (USAID 511-0655) to eliminate any cooperation or support to organizations that work in democracy and human rights.

Cuba: The regime prohibited international organizations to operate in the country. A representative from an organization funded by USAID is in jail due to Cuba's government claims that he was conspiring to provide funds to local Jewish groups.

Ecuador: At the moment there are no specific barriers, but there is a bill/statute under discussion that would regulate international organizations and international cooperation. The idea is that the state will guide the investment of funds available to these entities and decide how to manage the funds and in which activities they will be allowed to participate.

Venezuela: The government and the justice system (controlled by the president) have been persecuting, harassing, and using the court system against organizations with international support, and also expelling from the country representatives from Human Rights Watch and from religious groups.[18] The "Law for the Defense of Political Sovereignty and National Self-Determination," passed in December 2010, prohibits "organizations that defend political rights" from receiving international funding, in violation of Venezuela's own Constitution and international human rights commitments.

Barriers to Operational Activity

Direct (broadly-worded) prohibitions against spheres of activity:

Bolivia: NGOs are restricted from engaging in any human rights activities; governmental approval is required for any political gathering. Bolivia's government requested international donors to stop any funding to CSOs that work in human rights or democracy areas.

Ecuador: There are very vague prohibitions such as CSOs may be liable if they offend public order, which is an undefined legal concept, or if the organization does not comply with regulatory requirements. The government closed an environmental NGO just because it was opposed to a non-environmentally friendly project in the Ecuadorian Amazon area.

Cuba: Any activity considered by the regime as counter-revolutionary has been persecuted. Several countries prohibit participation in "extremist" activity against the "National Security" or "terrorist" activity without clearly defining these terms, thus allowing the state to block NGO activity in legitimate spheres.

Venezuela: Under the Law for the Defense of Political Sovereignty and National Self-Determination nongovernmental organizations that "defend political rights" or "monitor the performance of public bodies" are barred from receiving any foreign funding.

---

18 Venezuela's Supreme Tribunal (Constitutional Chamber) (Justice Cabrera) Decisions No. 656 (20/11/2000) and No. 1395 (21/11/2000): "Civil Society and NGOs cannot be funded, represented, associated, affiliated or supported directly or indirectly by international organizations, other states or governments or international movements. All the organizations must cooperate with the state and the government."

Invasive supervisory oversight: The government has the right to intervene in NGO operations, including membership by vetoing members, or introducing members of its own choice. Some governments restrict registered CSO activities regularly and continuously; failure to comply with these governmental demands leads to sanctions and penalties.

Nicaragua: State interference in associational activities is authorized by law; government representatives may attend association meetings and associations are required to obtain permission to undertake most activities.

Venezuela: Pressure is on national and international donors to reduce or eliminate support to Venezuelan NGOs. There are restrictions on permits to raise funds, to gain access to tax exemptions (only NGOs within the education area and limited by the decision of the tax authority), and government officials require bank owners to provide all the information of accounts, transactions, and data of NGOs, democracy leaders, and human rights activists.

Bolivia and Ecuador: Government controls the activities of organizations by authorizing registration authorities to audit their activities and finances and request any of the organization's documents at any time.[19]

Harassment from Government Officials: Government officials target opposition and NGOs to impede their activities:

Nicaragua: The government persecutes and harasses human rights and democracy leaders and organizations. The government and its followers have been attacking women's rights groups, destroying their installations, and prosecuting their leaders.[20]

Bolivia: Intrusive tax inspections of NGOs and burdensome report requirements. Government actions also created self-censorship.

Ecuador: The Civil Society Organizations have an obligation to provide any information that may be required by the authorities and facilitate access to government officials to carry out physical checks. The government uses its power to engage in continuous "courtesy" visits to opposition groups or CSOs that work in democracy, human rights, or the environment.

Venezuela: The Inter-American Human Rights Commission admitted a case that claims that the government created the "Maisanta" list with oppositionists and critics of the regime as a "blacklist" to deny jobs and public services, and to harass critics.[21]

---

19 Elements of Freedom of Association: A. The Right to Establish an Association with Legal Personality. This includes the Right to Registration required in order for an NGO to attain legal personality; B. The Right to Join (Or Not to Join) an Organization; C. The Right to Request, Obtain and Manage Licit Financial Resources; D. The Right to Affiliate with Other National and International Organizations; E. The Duty of the governments to avoid Unreasonable Interference in Internal Governance. Source: The Neglected Right: Freedom of Association in International Human Rights Law

20 The Centre for Communications Research, Five, the Autonomous Women's Movement, MAM, Oxfam Great Britain, the Civil Coordinator, Venezia Group, and the Network of Women in Local Matagalpa are the NGOs to which the District Judge II of Assizes sent a search warrant. The Attorney General of the Republic was accompanied by police to seize all administrative documentation and accounting records. END (El Nuevo Diario) October 10, 1908

21 People who are not close to the government suffered from exclusion, denial of public services, blocking from jobs, denials of passports and IDs, and other restrictions by the regime. Some organizations, like Cofavic, Una Ventana a la Libertad, Observatorio Ciudadano, and several journalists, have been opening

Criminal Penalties Against Individuals Associated with an Organization: Individuals who are found responsible for certain NGO activities can be held criminally liable and fined or imprisoned, which discourages NGO participation.

Venezuela: "Suspended" sentences against civil society activists are used to avoid international condemnation for imprisoning activists, while simultaneously discouraging them from future activism.[22]

Ecuador: The executive branch represented by the President attacked all the NGOs that have to do with the protests of the indigenous people against the water law project and threatened to sue them.

Cuba: A human rights campaigner was arrested while meeting in 2009 with local civil society representatives and was reportedly charged with espionage. Opposition or any activity to promote democracy is paid with jail time. More than 50 years of tyranny and repression.

Nicaragua: The courts (controlled by the government) have been opening cases against civil society organization leaders and opposition leaders. Recently the court suspended, with an unconstitutional procedure and decision, parliamentary immunity to opposition deputies and members of the congress, to force them to vote in favor of the authoritarian regime.

Lack of Independent Institutions, Rule of Law or Access to Remedies Against Restrictions or Attacks:

Venezuela: President Chávez controls the five branches of government[23] set out in Venezuela's constitution — executive, legislative, judicial, and the so-called "citizens' power" (which includes the Attorney General and the Accounting Office)[24]

Nicaragua: The government controls all the institutions and appointed judges from among the friends of the president, and President Daniel Ortega has been ruling by decree.[25]

Arbitrary or Discretionary Termination and Dissolution: Some governments use their significant discretion to shut down CSOs and use it to quash opposition groups.

---

procedures at the Inter American Human Rights Courts due to their fear for their lives and persecution from the regime. The government opened several trials against CSO activists and journalists. The government sent its "political" police forces to permanent "courtesy" visits to CSOs.

22 Criminal Code Reform Proposal: Any person or institution that provides, receives or distributes national or international funds or resources to conspire against the integrity of the republic or its institutions or disestablish our social order will be punished with 20 to 30 years in jail. Several democracy activists, students, and journalist are in jail or with an open court process due to their opinions or activities. The National comptroller has been imposing illegal restrictions for political participation to political leaders and NGO leaders. The President has been ordering open criminal procedures against CSO leaders and journalists. A judge is in jail just because the president ordered it.

23 Legislative, Judiciary, Executive, Moral and Electoral

24 Most notably he has centralized his control over the Supreme Court, which last year he expanded and packed with loyalists, the lower courts; the National Electoral Council (CNE),(four of whose five members are government supporters); the National Assembly, where all Deputies are appointed by the President (absolute control); and the office of the Attorney General. This is also true of the military, oil companies, and bank system.

25 The government of Daniel Ortega controls the Supreme Court and his rulings by decree have been oriented to take control of all the institutions.

Ecuador: New legislation gave broad power to the government to dissolve any organization, including the OSC, when it repeatedly violates the provisions issued by the ministries or agencies of control and regulation.[26]

Argentina: Even though this country is not part of the Alba, it has been moving toward authoritarian behavior. The law permits the termination of an NGO when it is "necessary" or "in the best interests of the public."[27]

Nicaragua: Several civic organizations have been arbitrarily terminated.[28] The government also eliminated the registration of several political groups and parties without any legal procedure.

Establishment of "Parallel" Organizations: Governments form or control their own CSOs (GONGOs) in order to undermine, discredit, and attract funding away from the legitimate CSO sector.

Bolivia: The government sponsored and funded a group of "parallel" organizations to compete with opposition CSOs; some of those groups are funded by the Venezuelan government.

Nicaragua: The government has established GONGOs with the aim of monitoring the activities of independent CSOs (GONGOs attend conferences and report on the activities of CSOs).[29] The government created the Citizens Power Councils as a way of societal control.[30]

Ecuador: The Government established a Secretariat of Peoples with the rank of Minister, to represent civil society and indigenous peoples and local peasants. This body organizes the agendas and activities and even gets to direct international funds to benefit these groups with government's views; they seldom consider the NGOs who think differently.

Cuba: The government created parallel unions and NGOs to block other organizations at the United Nations and International Workers Organizations.

Venezuela: The regime has been funded through "Missions" and developed a broad base of parallel-governmental organizations to "balance" NGOs. The government has been trying to create parallel CSOs in any area to counterbalance the activities of serious NGOs at the national and international levels, and block these organizations in their work in multilateral, regional, or global forums.

---

26 This implies an excess of discretion, and that determines what kind of provisions would configure the grounds for such dissolution. This argument was used by the government to settle the dissolution of the Ecological Action Corporation, which was made by Ministerial Agreement No. 0157 of March 5, 2009, arguing that that corporation had failed to fulfill the purposes for which it was constituted. This solution was later rescinded under an appeal lodged by the Corporation, but the legislation remains in force and has been supplemented by a new regulation (Ministerial Agreement No. 004) that determines a system of compliance control by the Ministries before declarations of this type.

27 "Defending Civil Society" supra note 6

28 "Defending Civil Society" supra note 6

29 "Recent Laws", supra note 10.

30 The Citizens' Power Councils (CPC) does not work as a NGO; however, they intend to do much of the work done by NGOs social involvement in community activity, financed with funds channeled through the CPC. In reality, the CPC was created by the government of Daniel Ortega as "a body of direct democracy." But what the public says is that the CPC is a political instrument of government, handled with state resources, and that only favors certain sectors of the population allied to the ruling party, or who are forced to accept its conditions for the benefits offered. It is a replica of the Sandinista Defense Committees (CDS), created in the eighties, during the first Sandinista government.

Lack of Protection: Governments try to avoid direct harassment against NGOs, but it doesn't provide for any protection for democracy or human rights activists.

Colombia: Even though Colombia is not an Alba country, there have been several claims about killings and harassments against union leaders and human right activists without proper investigation

Bolivia: Threats have been made against NGO leaders without any judicial order or legal base.

Ecuador: All the individuals and groups have constitutional rights and access to diverse procedures to defend them from the arbitrariness of the government authorities. Unfortunately, some organizations specialist in the area like the Center of Society and Law (Cides) there is no judicial independence to support the State of Law.

Venezuela: The government controls police and military forces and allows any violence against civil society activists or journalists. Followers of the government have been attacking media, CSOs, and leaders. This information has been documented and presented to the authorities but there has been no action or process against the violent perpetrators. The government uses the military and the police forces to repress intimidate, and persecute pacifist demonstrators.

Nicaragua: Daniel Ortega's government has been gradually undermining the institutionalization of the National Police, to the point that this body of public defense against crime behaves in an arbitrary manner. Violent groups funded by the government generate violence against CSOs and opposition leaders.[31]

Barriers to Speech and Advocacy: Limitations upon free speech, public policy engagement, and advocacy can severely limit NGOs' effectiveness.[32]

Prior restraints and censorship/burdens on publication:

Bolivia: The government supervises all the printing materials that need exonerations and impose censorship.

Venezuela: Any documentary, printing material, or information that can be perceived by the regime as dangerous or against the "revolution" can be destroyed and the TV channel, publisher, and newspaper can be fined or have their license suspended.[33] The Law for Social Responsibility in Radio, Television and Electronic

---

31 Police did not stop the attackers of the peaceful demonstrations. On the contrary, they permitted them to attack the citizenry who participated in the marches of the civil society or opposition political parties. On November 18, 2008, three radio stations in the city of León Orteganism were destroyed by mobs. When Juan José Toruño came to the radio, he found two policemen, yet they did nothing to prevent vandalism. The police said they had orders not to act. On December 10, 2008, in a mob attack against a peaceful march by the Orteganism for Human Rights, organized by the Nicaraguan Center for Human Rights (CENIDH) and the Civil Coordinator, strengthening police appeared several minutes after the initiation of aggression, , and forced the demonstrators to withdraw from the site. The Director of Defense and Withdrawal of CENIDH, Gonzalo Carrión, rejected the actions of the National Police, saying that this was, once again, uncooperative behavior to prevent the attack on the demonstrators. (The Press December 11, 2008)

32 "Defending Civil Society" supra note 6

33 The government prohibit any information from the NGO Cedice about property rights and also prohibits campaigns that include the president or his administration.

Media[34], a revised version of the existing broadcasting law, extends existing restrictions on free speech to the internet for the first time, with restrictions to messages that can be distributed by electronic media and provide government broadcasting authority, CONATEL, the authority to order internet service providers to restrict access to websites that contain expressions deemed to violate what the government views as messages that "foment anxiety in the public or disturb public order," "incite or promote disobedience of the current legal order," "refuse to recognize the legitimately constituted authority," or "incite or promote hatred or intolerance."

Defamation laws: Laws regarding defamation are used to hinder free speech and protect powerful people from scrutiny.[35]

Nicaragua: Defamation remains a criminal offence for which suspects can be arrested, and subject to hefty fines or imprisonment.[36]

Ecuador: All the individuals and groups have constitutional rights and access to diverse procedures to defend them from the arbitrariness of the government authorities. Unfortunately there is no judicial independence.

Venezuela: Laws enacting defamation were passed during 2005-2007 and several journalists were taken to court or jail. A journalist (Azocar) spent one year in jail for defamation against one of the officials of the regime. The court system is frequently used to harass members from the opposition or leaders from civil society.

Use of the Justice System and Institutions:

Venezuela: Supreme Tribunal (Tribunal Supremo) has been implementing decisions against NGOs and Civil Society (defining the concept of civil society).There have been 2670 trials and judicial procedures against NGOs, NGO leaders, human rights activists, journalists, and others. The Venezuelan Government use of the Attorney General/National Prosecutor Office (Fiscalia General) to treat and persecuting, political leaders, and activists. Administrative procedures have been used against NGOs. The Comptroller General (Contraloria General) has been opening cases against NGO leaders.[37]

Nicaragua: The government uses the judicial system to persecute opposition leaders and CSOs (women's groups among others), and the President has been using illegal decrees to keep his friends in the Supreme Court and other courts.

---

34 Approved on December 20, 2010

35 "Defending Civil Society" supra note 6

36 This has been since mid-2007 when it came into force in the New Criminal Code. Five women members of the Citizens' Power Councils (CPC) felt harmed by a publication in the newspaper La Prensa that was titled "CPC licensed to beatings," (which is true), and Jaime sued Chamorro, Director of the newspaper, and Mr. Eduardo Enriquez, Managing Editor, under this criminal offense. Despite not meeting the requirements of the process as there was no mention of the applicants in the report, the judge condemned the press for libel based on Article. 173 that states: He who by any means attacks the honor, reputation, or dignity of a person, or makes known his faults or purely private or domestic services, or because of their dishonorable or immoral character are likely to be exposed to the animosity, hatred, ridicule or public scorn, commits the crime of libel. (Media Centre)

37 Defamation cases against journalists (Gustavo Azocar, Nelson Bocaranda, and Marianela Salazar) and conspirator cases against Journalists (Patricia Poleo).

Use of Government Ownership of Media Sources and Government Controlled Media:

Venezuela: The government uses nationally-controlled media (TV, newspapers and radio stations) to threaten and defame NGO leaders. It failed to renew licenses to the private sector and increased its media through confiscations. The government has been taking control of almost all the TV and radio stations, and has also been developing its own media structure, which is used to intimidate and persecute opposition leaders and members of CSOs.[38]

Nicaragua: The government has been taking control of the media and uses the same approach as in Venezuela. The government used Venezuela's fund provided by Chávez to acquire TV stations. Daniel Ortega's government already controls several radio and television stations.[39]

Ecuador: The government closed TV Amazonas and other radio stations due to their work protecting some indigenous groups. There is an abuse of the "cadenas nacionales" compulsory President public broadcasting, since any mass media that rejects to join the public program may be punished. The government controls five TV stations and has a public TV station so is concentrating its power over information.

Venezuela, Bolivia, Ecuador and Nicaragua: Government power is used to force TV and radio stations to cover ongoing speeches and long messages from the presidents or their propaganda.

Venezuela / Nicaragua: The governments use only pro-government media to publish public and government funded advertising.

Venezuela, Nicaragua and Bolivia (Voiceless Activists): Only 100% pro-government human rights activists have access to media sources. Any other human rights or democracy activist is denied access to information.

Legal Restrictions on Independent Media: One of the fundamental tools for CSOs is access to independent media. There is a direct link between freedom of association and freedom of expression. The governments from the Bolivarian Alliance have been restricting freedom of expression to eliminate dissidence and avoid any criticism

---

38 The government controls 168 radio stations, 3 of 5 National TV channel networks, 234 community radios, and hundreds of media sources. The government uses its power to intimidate journalist, human rights and democracy activists, and dissidents with programs like LA HOJILLA (The Razor) or Vea, among others.

39 . In fact, it recently acquired Channel 8, which had a program transmitted by Fernando Carlos Chamorro, and This Week Tonight, that maintained an editorial line of complaint against the abuses of the regime and also against corruption journalistic research. The goal was to silence the journalist but he chose to leave the channel. The government has not confirmed a new broadcast license for several television channels and radio stations but with the possibility of canceling their permits, they have taken a very cautious stand with the government. It is recognized that maintaining a professional and informative program is safe, but not those that are investigative and complaint oriented. On January 29, 2007, First Lady Rosario Murillo, through a letter addressed to the Minister of Finance and Public Credit, stated that all advertising and propaganda would be authorized by the Council of Communication and Citizenship of the Presidency of the Republic. This is led by her and was in place for all ministries. In the SIP, journalists reported that the distribution of official advertising as a reward or punishment works to influence editorial decisions and information policies of the media. (Media Centre), The November 18, 2008 armed mobs attacked and destroyed three radio stations of the Radio Corporation of the West, owned by Anibal Toruño. The action came after a local radio deejay León, of Radio Dario, invited people to peacefully demonstrate in the streets against "voter fraud." (Media Centre). Dario Radio, Stereo Radio, and Radio Pats were destroyed by mortars, guns, sticks, and tubes by supporters of the FSLN. Juan José Toruño, director of the Western Radio Corporation said the damage was large-- they broke into the offices, took accounting documents, and "disappeared". An employee of the radio identified the Sandinista deputy Filiberto Rodriguez as one of the masked men who participated in the attack on the radio. (La Prensa, November 19, 2008)

Venezuela: The government approved new legislations with ideological contents to limit and control ideological content in the media, Chavez's government issued the Radio and Television Social Responsibility Law (content control).

Ecuador: In accordance with the new Organic Law of Communication, the government will create the "Superintendence of Telecommunications and Media (appointed by the President) and its role will be monitor, audit, intervene and control (Censor) the Media (Art. 48).

Bolivia: The inclusion of a norm in the constitution requiring that information and opinions disseminated by the media "respect the principles of truthfulness and responsibility" could lead to arbitrary restrictions of freedom of the press if enacted into law.

Venezuela, Ecuador and Nicaragua: Use of governmental telecommunication bodies to control the media, to censor material and intimidate opposition.

Closure to TV or Radio Stations

Venezuela: The government arbitrarily closed in 2007 the major TV channel (Radio Caracas Television, RCTV), in 2009 closed 34 Radio Stations and in July 2010 threatened to close 29 more, the government also closed the regional TV channel TV Guayana and took control of the last independent TV channel (Globovision) in July 2010.

Ecuador: On 29 August 2009, President Rafael Correa requested that a new process be opened against TV station "Teleamazonas" so that it may be "definitively closed down". Ecuador's President also announced a process of "Nationalization" of radio and TV stations.

Nicaragua: Nicaragua's telecom regulator, Telcor, cancelled the frequency of Radio La Ley, in Sebaco (northern Nicaragua) (June 22, 2009). The station is owned by an opposition commentator openly against Daniel Ortega. The closure was carried out by 30 armed civilians who confiscated the station's broadcast equipment. The government announced the closure of five more Radio Stations.

Broad, vague restrictions against advocacy: Ambiguous terms are often used to restrict "political" or "extremist" activities, giving the government substantial discretion to punish those whose statements are deemed improper, that in turn serve to chill free expression.[40]

Nicaragua: The government continuously creates false claims and develops vague restrictions[41] against civil society organizations, activist and journalists.

---

40   "Defending Civil Society" supra note 6

41 On August 26, 2008, the director of Attention to Political Parties Supreme Electoral Council (CSE), Julio Acuna, filed a complaint for election offenses against the International Republican Institute (IRI), after the former president of Mexico, Vicente Fox, participated in a conference entitled "The state of democracy in Latin America", sponsored by the IRI. (The Press, Sep. 4, 2008). All educational and civic organizations involved in inviting the former president of Mexico, Vicente Fox, were cited by the prosecution to testify. On October 13, 2008, the president of Let Democracy, a member of the Latin American and Caribbean Network for Democracy, was summoned to testify as part of the "investigation conducted by the Public Prosecutor in accordance with the provisions on Art. 90 CPP and the Organic Law of Public Prosecutions. "

Venezuela: Any public act must be authorized by the government and the government supporters also intimidate and harass all the private demonstrations. The government has been creating "special zones" which are certain areas in which any kind of demonstration is not allowed (includes highways, public plazas, spaces near governmental buildings, and every place that they decide to consider "special"). Under the Law for the Defense of Political Sovereignty and National Self-Determination foreigners invited to Venezuela who provide critics to the regime will be summarily expelled from the country if they express opinions that "offend the institutions of state, top officials or attack the exercise of sovereignty." Organizations that invite them would face stiff fines, and their directors could lose their right to run for public office for up to eight years.

Ecuador: The Ecuadorian constitution indicates that all information must be truthful against the Inter-American human rights dispositions. In other words, the information may be controlled by the government in case of non-truthful information. Some public demonstrations need the previous authorization of the authority to express their opinion and the government denies those permits in a regular basis.

Bolivia: the government must authorize any public demonstration.

Cuba: Public demonstrations are not allowed and the government represses and persecutes any kind of advocacy.

Violence and Intimidation:

Venezuela: These actions come from Government Special Forces and Police Corps (DISIP, DIM, Military, PTJ, Police Corps, Militia, Bolivarian Circles and Arm Government Supporters, Violent Parallel NGOs), including permanent and direct attacks from the Venezuelan President, his ministries, officials, and followers on NGOs and their leaders. A special list with names of NGO leaders, opposition leaders, and people who vote against the president is used to deny them access to information, documents, employment, and contract with the government (Lista de Tascon y Lista Maisanta) and to open trials against them. There is use of violent groups to attack CSOs leaders and opposition leaders. Several cases of persecution against CSO leaders and use of commando groups to intimidate them have been reported. The violent group called La Piedrita attacked media sources (RCTV, Globovision, Ultimas Noticias).

Nicaragua: Direct violence against journalists and media owners was justified by the regime. Kidnapping, extortion, and daily violence are the norm.[42]

Bolivia: Dozens of journalists were assaulted in 2008 and 2009 while covering protests. One journalist was killed during a local civic dispute in 2008. Pro government groups generally attacked private media outlets and their reporters, while antigovernment groups focused their attacks on government-controlled media. There is also use of paid supporters to intimidate opposition leaders.

---

42 The Office of the Special Rapporteur for Freedom of Expression of the Inter-American Commission on Human Rights (IACHR) on October 1, 2009, expressed its concern regarding the growing wave of attacks against media outlets and journalists in Ecuador, and called on the authorities to investigate these incidents. The Office received information on the threats received by several journalists, including Yamila Murillo Zaldúa, of Diario Correo, in the locality of Machala, and Aquiles Arismendi, of Radio La Voz de su Amigo, in the city of Esmeraldas.

Venezuela, Bolivia and Nicaragua: Government supporters sometimes physically attack journalists working for critical outlets. Recently a group of Sandinistas attacked a peaceful march in Managua and beat a journalist they accused of supporting the Honduran coup.

Presidential Attacks

Venezuela, Bolivia, Ecuador and Nicaragua: Presidents Chávez, Morales, Correa, and Ortega have been active opponents of civil society leaders, journalists and media owners. Chavez uses both his controlled media and forced messages in all the media to attack some CSO leaders directly. Morales often lambasts the private media for backing the opposition agenda and declares them his "enemies". Daniel Ortega wages personal war against Nicaraguan journalist and television anchor, Carlos Fernando Chamorro, and others. [43]

Restrictions on freedom of assembly: By making it difficult or even illegal for individuals and groups to gather or meet (i.e., to exercise freedom of assembly), the law directly hinders the ability of NGOs to plan or engage in advocacy activities. [44]

Paraguay: Paraguay is not part of this study but its president has becoming more close to Alba. Proposals are underway for the modification of the penal code and an Anti-Terrorist Law which could result in the criminalization of social protest. [45]

Venezuela: Intimidation and hearings by Congress Members and deputies for NGO leaders due to "conspirator" and other false allegations. The government uses its violent groups and police forces to intimidate any opposition meeting.

Bolivia: The government uses violent followers to repress and persecute opposition leaders and demonstrators.

Nicaragua: The government funds violent groups to intimidate and implement a violent response to any kind of democratic assembly. They have been persecuting and shooting congress leaders and CSOs.

Barriers to Contact and Communication: These restrictions impede the ability of NGOs to receive and provide information, and to meet and exchange ideas with their civil society counter-parts. [46]

Barriers to the creation of networks: Existing legal entities may be limited or even prohibited in their freedom to form groups, networks, coalitions, or federations. [47]

---

43 On October 11, 2008, a Nicaraguan federal prosecutor, Douglas Vargas, accompanied by a dozen armed police agents, raided the Managua offices of CINCO, a nonprofit journalism organization directed by Carlos Fernando Chamorro. Women's rights activist Sofía Montenegro offices were raided in October 2008 after she denounced Ortega for outlawing abortion in Nicaragua. There were direct attacks against La Prensa, El Nuevo Diario, Canal 2.

44 "Defending Civil Society" supra note 6

45 "Defending Civil Society" supra note 6

46 "Defending Civil Society" supra note 6

47 "Defending Civil Society" supra note 6

Venezuela: The government has been attacking organizations with international affiliations. At the Organization of American State, the United Nations, and other international organizations, the government has been trying to block Civil Society Organizations.

Ecuador: No barriers yet, but there is a real menace that within the communication law, access to the Internet and social networks may be restricted.

Bolivia: The government has simply refused to register umbrella groups.

Cuba: No networks are allowed in Cuba.

Nicaragua: The Director and Control Department of the Interior Ministry MIGOB, Gustavo Syria, accused the agencies with legal status as persons to, "have lent their name for these organisms are not registered to receive funding for a range of activities and amounts In the millions" [48]

Barriers to international contact: Governments prevent and inhibit international contact by controlling exit and entry to the country for nationals and internationals.[49]

Venezuela: The government does not renew passports for leaders from CSOs and in one case, retained the passport when the person returned to the country. There are specific controls on organizations that want to participate in international events. The government uses its diplomacy to attack organizations at the United Nations, Organization of American States, and other forums.

Cuba: There are restrictions to international contact and even Internet control.

Nicaragua: Government diplomats from Nicaragua began placing some basic restrictions to NGOs with international activities.

Barriers to access to Information:

Nicaragua and Venezuela: Only the Official media (TV, Radio, Newspapers, Communitarian media and other sources indentified 100% with the government or its political project) have access to official information. The government denied private media equal access to many official events, even in cases when private media had access to government facilities. Morales refused to engage with certain press outlets, on occasion naming specific reporters as enemies.

Self-Censorship:

Venezuela: The two last TV stations in the hand of private parties, Venevision and Televen, are controlled indirectly by the government with threats and governmental advertising.

Nicaragua and Venezuela: Terror and intimidation tactics against journalists and media owners.

---

48 The Press Sep 25, 2009

49   "Defending Civil Society" supra note 6

Use of Governmental Apparatus to Counter-Inform:

Venezuela: Development of thousands of web-pages, community media, "independent" journalists, and other forms of information used to promote the "revolution" and attack opposition (100 million dollar campaign per year).

Barriers to Resources: Some governments restrict the access of CSOs to foreign funding, ostensibly in order to reduce foreign influence.[50]

Prohibitions against certain categories of funding:

Bolivia: All funding must fulfill the priorities of the Government national plan and canalized by the government. By Presidential Decree the government established the requirement of previous approval from the Ministry of Planning and Development to allow any foreign organization to operate in Bolivia.[51]

Venezuela: Funding from the US is considered against the revolution and organizations that have received those funds have been persecuted, intimidated, harassed, and subject to criminal procedures for "conspiracy with the empire".

Advance government approval: More commonly, the law allows the receipt of foreign funding, but requires advance governmental approval.

Ecuador: Regulations that impose, among other things, reporting and approval mechanisms that give the government control over donor funds and projects. Foreign aid is heavily taxed.

Bolivia: The government requires pre-approval of funds and a deposit in favor of the government.

Routing Funding through the Government:

Bolivia: Requires all donor funds to flow through government ministries, allowing NGOs to receive funding only if they develop activities according to governmental plans. In 2009, the government began requiring that foreign funding for NGOs be channeled through government-controlled banks, thereby allowing the monitoring of all money transfers, and affording the opportunity to extract part of the money transfer, whether through administrative fees, taxation, or corruption. CSOs must deposit in governmental accounts a percentage of the funds received directly for their activities.

Ecuador: The NGOs Law project presents some threats in this regard.

Venezuela: The government implemented an exchange control mechanism that made illegal any form of foreign money transfer not controlled directly by the government.

---

50 "Recent Laws", supra note 10

51 The government also signed an agreement with the US government (USAID 511-0655) to eliminate any cooperation or support to organizations that work in democracy and human rights. The priorities for the government are infrastructure projects. Since the Ministry of Planning and Development controls all the funding for Bolivia (grants and cooperation), the government just restricts funding for democracy and human rights.

Use of Taxing/Fiscal Authority:

Venezuela: Sanctions and fiscal persecution to media owners, media outlets (Globovision) and also denied tax exceptions to CSOs. The government also opened procedures against CSOs and media outlets.

Nicaragua: Elimination of tax benefits (Arce Law).

Currency Exchange Control:

Venezuela: Since the government implemented an exchange and currency control in 2004 that only allows currency exchange from local currency to dollars or Euros in controlled circumstances, there has been the creation of a black market for dollars.[52]

The information included in this research and document came from questionnaires and interviews to experts and practitioners in Venezuela, Cuba, Ecuador, Bolivia and Nicaragua, as well as some experts that work at the regional level. In the interviews, the questions include also a review of the impacts of these restrictions in the daily activities and work of the organizations, how have these measures affected the way NGOs and democracy leaders in the Alba countries operate. A common view and similar impacts were found in the responses. Here are the most common impacts:

a. Fear and continuous pressure from the government.
b. Stigmatization.
c. Some US officials and administrative personnel in charge of US funds do not want to work with some NGOs due to the risk of being deported from the country. Some other countries have also taken the same approach.
d. Some programs must be implemented in the shadow of the law.
e. Reduction of the number and size of CSOs.
f. Polarization of several NGO leaders.
g. Limited ability to work.
h. Fear environment (Threatens leaders and personnel).
i. More personal and family risks.
j. General bias against NGOs due to official campaigns.
k. Operational risk.
l. Lack of possibilities for medium or long term planning.
m. Lack of funding; donors are afraid and there are less international and national resources.
n. More effort and time devoted to defending the institution and its personnel.
o. Lack of access to public documents, sources, information, and limitation to participate.

---

52 The government controls how many dollars it allows to exchange per person and per industry and that is an effective form of control against the free media. Since exchanging and trading dollars in the black market is illegal, and the newspapers and magazines need official approval for dollars to buy paper, ink, and other basic components, the government uses this tool to pressure printed media and other media sources.

p.   Cost of legal defense, administrative procedure costs, and lawyers.
The lack of private, public, and international financing for human rights and democracy NGOs in the Alba region continually makes it more difficult to achieve a democratic balance.

What we can see in common in the Alba Countries?

To illustrate current patterns and common restrictions in Alba countries against freedom of assembly, freedom of operation and freedom of speech this study took all the categories of restrictions and tabulated the findings for each country. We assigned a value of 0 when the country didn't use certain restriction and 1 one when we found some cases of limitations or actions against CSOs or independent media.

Common Trends in the Alba Countries Against CSOs					
I. Barriers to Entry					
	Bolivia	Cuba	Ecuador	Venezuela	Nicaragua
Limited Rights to Associate and Form NGOs	0	1	1	1	1
Prohibitions against unregistered groups	0	1	0	1	1
Restrictions on founders	1	1	1	1	1
Inability to register and secure the benefits registration	1	1	1	1	1
Vague grounds for denial of registration	1	1	1	1	1
Re-registration requirements	0	0	1	1	0
Barriers for international organizations	1	1	1	1	0
TOTAL (7)	**4**	**6**	**6**	**7**	**5**

II. Barriers to Operational Activity					
	Bolivia	Cuba	Ecuador	Venezuela	Nicaragua
Direct (broadly-worded) prohibitions against spheres of activity	1	1	1	0	0
Invasive supervisory oversight	1	1	1	1	1
Harassment from Government Officials	1	1	1	1	1
Criminal Penalties Against Individuals Associated with an Organization	0	1	1	1	1
Lack of Independent Institutions, Rule of Law or Access to Remedies	0	1	0	1	1
Arbitrary or Discretionary Termination and Dissolution	0	1	1	0	1

Establishment of "Parallel" Organizations	1	1	1	1	1
Lack of Protection	1	1	1	1	1
TOTAL (8)	**5**	**8**	**7**	**6**	**7**

III. Barriers to Speech and Advocacy					
	Bolivia	Cuba	Ecuador	Venezuela	Nicaragua
Prior restraints and censorship/burdens on publication	1	1	0	1	0
Defamation laws	0	1	1	1	1
Use of the Justice System and Institutions	0	1	0	1	1
Use of Government Controlled Media	0	1	1	1	1
Legal Restrictions to Independent Media	1	1	1	1	0
Closure to TV or Radio Stations	0	1	1	1	1
Broad, vague restrictions against advocacy	1	1	1	1	1
Violence and Intimidation	1	1	0	1	1
Presidential Attacks	1	1	1	1	1
Restrictions on freedom of assembly	1	1	0	1	1
TOTAL (10)	**6**	**10**	**6**	**10**	**8**

IV. Barriers to Contact and Communication					
	Bolivia	Cuba	Ecuador	Venezuela	Nicaragua
Barriers to the creation of networks	1	1	1	1	1
Barriers to international contact	0	1	0	1	1
Access to Information	0	1	0	1	1
Self Censorship	0	1	0	1	1
Use of Governmental Apparatus to Counter-Inform	0	1	0	1	0
TOTAL (5)	**1**	**5**	**1**	**5**	**4**

V. Barriers to Resources					
	Bolivia	Cuba	Ecuador	Venezuela	Nicaragua
Prohibitions against certain categories of funding	1	1	0	1	0
Advance government approval	1	1	1	0	0
Routing Funding through the Government	1	1	1	1	0
Use of Taxing/Fiscal Authority	0	1	0	1	1
Exchange Control	0	1	0	1	0
TOTAL (5)	**3**	**5**	**2**	**4**	**1**

Comparative View					
	Bolivia	Cuba	Ecuador	Venezuela	Nicaragua
Barriers to Entry	4	6	6	7	5
Barriers to Operational Activity	5	7	7	6	7
Barriers to Speech and Advocacy	6	10	6	10	8
Barriers to Contact and Communication	1	5	1	5	4
Barriers to Resources	3	5	2	4	1
TOTAL (35)	19	33	22	32	25

This study included thirty five (35) different barriers, laws, policies, and practices that stifle the work of civil society organizations and independent media. There is a clear pattern among all the countries in terms of the violations. In the case of Cuba, a dictatorial regime, the restrictions and controls exceed the rest of the Alba countries, followed by Venezuela with 32/35 limitations against freedom of association or expression. Venezuela, Cuba and Nicaragua exhibited the worst behavior against civil society organizations and freedom of association and expression.

According to Salomon (1999), there are great similarities in the countries that have enacted or proposed laws that restrict the activities of civil society organizations (CSOs). Such countries tend to exhibit one or more of the following characteristics[53]:

A. They have a 'closed' or command economy (Venezuela, Cuba) or are governed by leaders with autocratic tendencies (Nicaragua, Bolivia).
B. There is political dissension in the country or a neighboring country that is perceived as threatening the current regime or incumbent party (Venezuela with Colombia and the US).
C. There are concerns about religious fundamentalism (does not apply in Latin America).
D. Similar legislation or practices have been introduced elsewhere in the region (all the Alba countries). In some cases this almost amounts to an 'exchange of worst practices'.
E. They have a history of human rights abuses (Nicaragua, Venezuela, and Bolivia).
F. They are concerned about 'foreign involvement' (Venezuela, Bolivia, and Nicaragua).

We can see a clear pattern of persecution and restrictions against Civil Society Organizations and independent media in Venezuela, Cuba, Bolivia, and Nicaragua, and increasing control and limitations in Ecuador.

---

53 Excerpted from Global Civil Society: Dimensions of the Nonprofit Sector, Lester M. Salamon, et. al., Johns Hopkins Center for Civil Society Studies, 1999

While the ALBA countries do not share all the characteristics above, there is a clear pattern of the restrictions above against Civil Society Organizations and independent media in Venezuela, Cuba, Bolivia, and Nicaragua and increasing control and limitations in Ecuador. The Limitations and persecution are in place in all of the countries, with the most severe impacts in Cuba, Venezuela and Nicaragua.

Part II: Comparative Civil Society Regulation in Latin America

Is it desirable to have a very comprehensive general legislation governing civil society?, Is there a need a comprehensive law regulating civil society organizations (CSOs) and their activities? Is it wise to compile all laws related to civil society in single legal framework—a detailed, all-encompassing association law for instance? Should there be different laws for different types of CSOs? None of these questions have easy answers, and answering each of them depends on each country's specific situation. In some countries the simplicity of the registration system facilitates the functioning of civil society organizations, enabling civil society to register they by-laws and operate freely it is a fundamental freedom. Establishing a comprehensive legal framework to govern CSOS has the advantage of aggregating scattered laws to provide greater coherence and the opportunity to create a clear, concise determination of the appropriate relationship between the state and civil society. However, on the other hand, the drafting of such a law also provides governments the opportunity to further restrict civil society. Additionally, sometimes it is not appropriate to draft one large legal framework to govern a variety of associations; for instance, unions, neighborhood organizations, charity foundations, etc., are all quite different in their aim and operations. Here, the sociopolitical context of the country becomes very important. Venezuela demonstrates this point well. It would be ridiculous for a government like that in Venezuela, which actively persecutes civil society organizations and their leaders, to draft a comprehensive law on association. = In fact, resistance to Venezuela's efforts to pass a law on cooperation proved to be a positive development. However, in countries like Costa Rica, which has a series of obsolete laws embedded in civil codes dating back up to two centuries, a comprehensive law has the advantage of bringing into force a modern legal regime that could actually empower civil society.

After completing analysis of legislation and regulatory structures addressing civil society in many Latin American countries, as well as the reality on the ground, the situation of civil society in many countries is disappointing. Countries with greater economic and political stability have the highest respect for the civil society organizations, in countries with more authoritarian regimes the government persecutes civil society organizations.

Limits to Freedom of Association of Civil Society Organizations in Latin America

Country	Regulatory Environment (clear regulations and laws)	and barriers to entry	Follow up system	Time for Registration	Freedom of operation for International Organizations	Limits to Activities	Limits to funding	Limits to communication	Tax benefits	Government Power to Control and Dissolve	Total
Argentina	5	5	5	4	5	4	5	3	5	5	46
Bolivia	4	3	3	4	2	3	2	2	4	2	29
Brazil	5	5	5	5	5	5	5	5	5	5	50
Chile	5	5	5	5	5	5	5	5	5	5	50
Colombia	5	5	5	5	5	3	5	4	5	5	47
Costa Rica	4	3	3	2	2	3	5	5	4	3	34
Cuba	3	0	0	3	0	0	0	0	0	0	6
Ecuador	2	2	3	2	3	2	1	2	2	1	20
El Salvador	4	5	5	4	5	4	5	5	4	3	44
Guatemala	4	3	4	5	3	3	5	5	5	2	39
Honduras	4	4	4	4	4	4	4	4	4	3	39
Mexico	5	3	4	5	4	4	5	5	4	5	44
Nicaragua	2	2	3	3	3	2	3	2	4	2	26
Panama	4	3	4	4	4	2	5	5	4	3	38
Paraguay	3	3	3	3	5	3	5	5	5	5	40
Peru	4	4	4	5	4	5	3	5	4	3	41
Dominican Republic	4	4	4	5	5	5	5	3	5	4	44
Uruguay	5	4	5	4	5	4	5	4	5	4	45
Venezuela	1	2	2	1	2	0	0	0	1	2	11

Methodology: A questionnaire was distributed among 293 individuals and organizations and we received 178 filled questionnaires from Civil Society Organizations and experts from all the countries in Latin America. The answers were tabulated and evaluated and the data helped to elaborate a comparative review and chart. The questionnaire also included a poll about freedom for civil society organizations to operate in each country. The answers to the questionnaires and the poll helped to develop a comparative chart assigning a value from 0-5, 0 the worst indicator and 5 the best.

In my study, Cuba fares by far the worst in terms of freedom of associate, no doubt a function of its overall failure to provide for human rights and fundamental freedoms. Even when Cuban law allows for the registration of a civil society organization, its freedom to operate is severely limited. Another serious case is Venezuela. In December 2010, Venezuela adopted the Law on Political Sovereignty, grossly impeding the activities of human rights and democracy organizations to associate, assemble, and speak on issues of public importance.

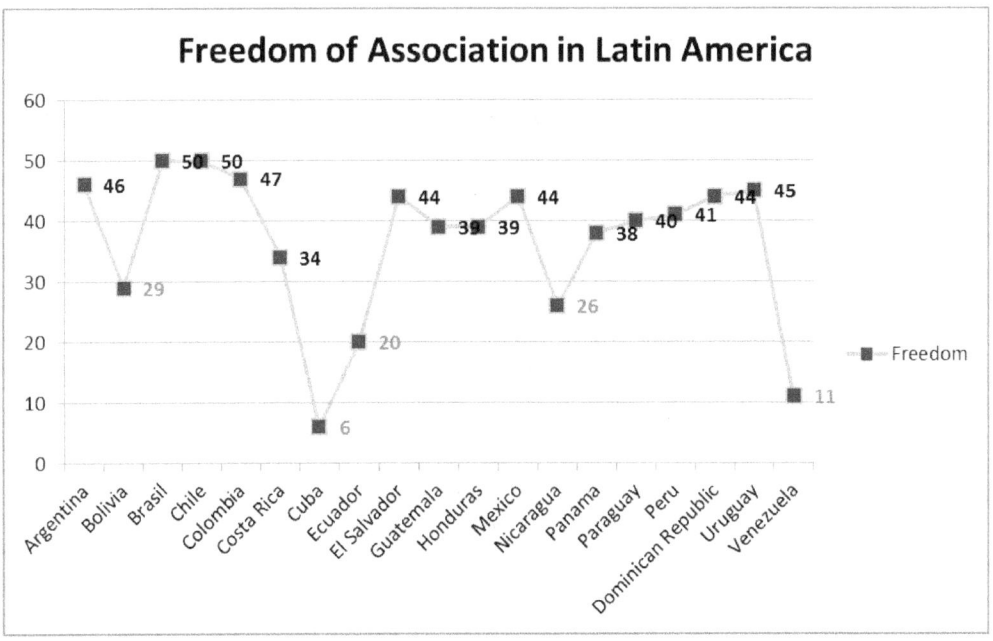

Aggregating data I collected in my research, the above graph reveals that democracy and transparency correspond with freedom of association for civil society organizations. The Alba countries fared worst in terms of having fair mechanisms for registration, as well as in respecting freedoms of operation, of assembly, and of expression.

Bolivia, Ecuador and Nicaragua did not rate well either. Ecuador has also increased controls, regulations, and limitations on civil society. In the case of Nicaragua, civil society organizations face direct and indirect persecution from the government.

Costa Rica, a country that would seem amenable to civil society, also has problems. Legislation requires hinders civil society organizations ability to register by mandating that a government official be involved in the process. Meanwhile, in Peru, a strong regulatory system tightly controls civil society, and government officials are intent to pass even more restrictions.

Some countries, e.g. Argentina, Uruguay and El Salvador, require an initial investment of more than $ 1,000 to register an organization.

Several organizations complained of the lack of support and solidarity from democracy-focused CSOs in democratic countries.

In April 2011, Honduras passed an association law that regulates Development Non Governmental Organizations (ONGD) and even when it places new controls on civil society groups, including a minimum number of members an organization can have (7), a prohibition on family members' participation in the same organization restrictions on how organizations manage funds, and an allowance for the government to close an organization with which it disagrees, this law it is better than the previous one and the regalement can improve the legislation, but it is a good initiative.

In the research, only Chile and Brazil showed high levels of freedom of association and of operation for civil society organizations. Brazil has an online system to register NGOs that is quite easy to use and imposes no limitations in terms of NGOs funding, communication, or operations. Additionally, contributions from donors to registered CSOs are tax-deductible. In Chile, organizations are registered within a two month timeframe following their application. The Chilean government has established a civil society fund to strengthen civil society and allows individual and corporate donors to deduct contributions to CSOs up to 5% of the donor's annual income. Colombia also has a streamlined registration process in which NGO registration can take place in less than 24 hours and not involve the Chamber of Commerce. Additionally, Colombia too has instituted tax-friendly policies toward NGOs, including tax exemptions and tax incentives for donors. However, on the other hand, the attacks ton civil society organizations experienced during the previous government and threats posed by violent groups creates limitations on the freedom of Colombian civil society to operate and on its leaders to express themselves freely.

CSOs in Argentina, Mexico, and El Salvador also enjoy a degree of freedom not experienced in other countries in the hemisphere. All countries have fair registration systems and few restrictions on CSOs' operations. Registration in all these countries is online and free from repressive government control. All countries also enjoy tax exemption. However, registration, while easy, is not without its problems. In all of these countries, the cost to register an organization is exorbitant. According to interviewees, registration can cost more than $ 1,000. In Mexico and Argentina, there are also limits on the freedom of expression due to control of private media. Government restrictions reduce the ability of civil society organizations to operate. In El Salvador, the faculty in the hands of the Ministry of Government to dissolve a CSO due to illegal activities without a clear explanation of the process can be a factor that affects the operation of some organizations adverse to any tendency in power. In the case of Mexico, the government also allows CSOs to engage the state in foreign policy planning, a level of interaction with the state that is forbade in many Latin American countries.

In some countries like El Salvador, the Dominican Republic, and Honduras, CSOs are automatically registered if the registration authority has not granted a decision in three months. A majority of countries have a centralized system to register CSOs and manage a database to keep track of them.

After reviewing and analyzing data, we found clear differences between countries in terms of how states control the operations of CSOs and the parameters in which they are permitted to operate. Most states limit the operations of CSOs by circumscribing their operations according to a legal requirement that the CSO not act contrary to morality or public order (Panama) or state security (Chile). These limitations on acceptable behavior give the government too much power to make determinations of what is "moral" and in "public order." The legal parameters in which an CSO is allowed to operate should be clear and precise; there should be no threat that broad and vague concepts such as "morality," "public order" or even "state security" could be used to delimit acceptable CSO activity. This is the case in Panama where there have been several cases in which the government has refused to register LGBT organizations on the ground that they are not in harmony with public morality.

In Venezuela, a Supreme Court decision illegalizes the receipt of funds from abroad. In other cases, law requires CSOs to operate in accordance with the "public interest" And a Law passed in December 2010 prohibits CSO from organizing or inviting someone who can criticized the government. Some countries use this requirement to deny NGOs the right to register and restrict their operations.

One of the key findings of this research is that many civil society leaders do not understand the balance between passing civil society laws that allow CSOs to freely register and operate, respecting freedoms of operation and of assembly, and the need to craft legislation to restrict organized criminal groups. In some cases, especially Colombia and Mexico, interviewees responded that they had "too much freedom," which allowed some organizations to be used as platforms for organized crime or corruption. However, narrow, well-defined legislation can be drafted to address criminal organizations, without jeopardizing legitimate CSOs free exercise of the right of association. This is probably best done in a country's criminal code, not in its association laws.

It is clear that the more democratic and open the country, the more free is its civil society.

Part III: Techniques applied by NGOs in restrictive scenarios to improve their work and become effective against the backlash

As part of this study, taking into account the recommendations from WMD's Defending Civil Society report and ICNL documents and research, a comprehensive set of tools has been developed to assist NGOs in Latin America in their effort for prevention and being protected from Human Rights violations, and restoration of respect for human rights.

Challenge Restrictions in domestic and international courts and Human Rights Systems

For regulation in the civil society sector, domestic laws can provide a juridical framework only if they increase participation and guarantee access to information. They must also respect freedoms of association, respect all the principles for protecting civil society and the independence of organizations and activists. Overall these laws should be in full compliance with the international obligations of the state in the field of human rights and fundamental freedoms.[vii] International human rights obligations are to be interpreted as comprising all treaty-based and customary law obligations of the state, as well as human rights standards adopted within the United Nations system and by regional human rights bodies.[viii]

Domestic Litigation

In countries where the courts are reasonably independent and fair, domestic litigation is an effective way for NGOs to challenge legislative provisions that unduly restrict their operations. This approach is not effective in all countries, however, and even where effective, may consume extreme amounts of time and resources. Finally, there are some countries in which going through domestic courts is simply a way to fulfill the requirement of exhausting domestic options before petitioning an international tribunal.[ix]

Litigation before International Tribunals

International tribunals have the mandate of protecting basic human rights guaranteed by international conventions. For example, CSOs in the Americas have been using the Inter American Human Rights System as a way to protect organizations and activists and also to bring their cases to the international level. The Inter American System also provides an opportunity for dialogue among CSOs and governments.

National and International Human Rights Mechanisms

National Mechanisms: In many countries, internal governmental entities are charged with the responsibility to monitor or enforce human rights law. This includes ombudsmen, human rights/truth commissions, and judicial regulatory bodies. Depending on the context, filing complaints with these bodies can be effective.

International Human Rights Mechanisms: The right to freedom of association is protected by numerous international covenants and treaties. Various international human rights mechanisms exist in order to ensure that these international instruments are respected: The Human Rights Committee (established under the International Covenant on Civil and Political Rights)[x] accepts complaints and investigates human rights violations.[xi] The Special Representative of the UN Secretary General on Human Rights Defenders – established in 2000 to support the implementation of the 1998 Declaration on Human Rights Defenders, and to promote the rights set out in international human rights instruments, including the Universal Declaration and the ICCPR.[xii] The UN Commission on Human Rights has established mechanisms for human rights violations complaints.[xiii]

Regional Human Rights Mechanisms: The Inter-American Commission on Human Rights examines complaints or petitions regarding specific cases of human rights violations (violations of the Charter of the OAS and the American Convention on Human Rights).

Legal Triage

Programs that provide legal defense to civil society workers can be effective; for example, ICNL provides legal consultants in Central American countries to assist organizations in registering and in meeting other legal requirements.[xiv] Under the Pinochet dictatorship in Chile, the Vicariate of Solidarity, with the aid of the Catholic Church, provided legal defense services.[xv] In Venezuela the Asociacion Civil Consorcio Desarrollo y Justicia has been helping other CSOs to register their organizations in "safe" countries like Costa Rica, Panama, or the US.

Bilateral Investment Treaties ("BITs")[xvi]

An alternate and not so explored route to fight against NGO regulations is using the existing international regime governing economic activities, bilateral economic agreements, trade agreements, and mechanisms to protect foreign investments. Even when the goal and structure of these agreements and trade structures are not oriented to NGOs (they are designed for for-profits), it is possible to use them for protection of private property, protection of a specific activity, protection of non-profit investment in the specific country, claims for expropriation, breaches of the treaty obligation, and claims from limitations in the free flux of money, among other initiatives. According to a recent publication from The International Center for Not-for-Profit Law (2007), *International Investment Treaty Protection of Not-for-Profit Organizations*, the NGO sector can take advantage of more than 2500 BITs. When regimes interfere with transfers of international funds, deny registration or re-registration of NGOs with ties to international organizations or organizations in another country, or seizes assets of the NGO due to "NGO Laws." These organizations can claim breaches of contract or they can challenge with trade guarantees, like free transfer of capital, fair and equitable treatment, full protection and security, and national treatment and avoid interference. In addition, there is also the possibility to use free trade dispute resolution systems. [xvii]

Challenge Legislation and defend basic principles

Use distraction techniques, delays and volunteer to be part of the discussions: In some countries, like Mexico, NGOs prevented stricter regulations in the legislative and policy making procedure and recommended alternatives. NGOs must always appear as open to dialogue. In Peru, NGOs helped the government develop regulations, but only for the use of public funds. When scandals arise in the United States, not-for-profits always initiate the process of self regulation to prevent claims for stricter regulations. In Mexico, a common effort among NGOs, academia, and the government produced positive changes in regulations to the not-for-profit sector.

Promote new regional tools

Use Regional mechanisms to look for better ways to protect civil society. NGOs can use regional structures and negotiation abilities to promote better environments for civil society at the regional levels, and with that put some pressure in their own countries.

In the Americas, the Latin American Network for Democracy, the network Democracia Activa, DPLF, FH and Cejil in a coordinated effort with the governments of United States, Canada, Colombia, Chile and Guatemala developed and negotiated a new resolution at the Organization of American States (OAS) for the Promotion of the Rights to Freedom of Assembly and of Association in the Americas (AG/RES 2680 XLI-O/11) and it was approved by the OAS General Assembly in El Salvador. This Resolution includes for the first time freedom of association as a fundamental right in the region. This effort proves that a good coordination among governments and civil society can produce changes at the international level.

Campaigns to stop the regulations

When a regulation has only passed one of the approval stages, it is the perfect time to develop strategic planning and try to stop the regulation, using all the tools reflected in this document. An effective campaign from more than 117 Venezuelan NGOs stopped the "Cooperation Law" with the help of the international community, Canada's Government, NED, INCL, European Union country embassies, and other actors.

Law Reform Campaigns

CSOs and their partners can work to sponsor progressive domestic legislation governing their formation, operation, and sustainability. While this may be possible in states that show a trend towards liberalization, it may be particularly difficult in states that are actively oppressing civil society.[xviii] This has been effective in Peru, and in Mexico.

Legislation to "organize" civil society or cooperation

NGOs must fight to avoid any attempt at passing such legislation. At the very least the need is to "Protect Fundamental Freedoms". The following elements must be necessary in the legislation governing CSOs or NGOs in order to ensure that fundamental freedoms of association, expression, and peaceful assembly are respected:

Creation of a CSO: CSOs should be allowed to freely come into existence; also, CSOs should not be required to obtain legal standing in order to engage in lawful activities.

Registration (or Incorporation) of CSOs: Registration should be quick, easy, and inexpensive for all persons (natural and legal).

Registration or Incorporation Organization: State organization responsible for giving legal existence to CSOs should be adequately staffed, even-handed; decisions not to register a CSO should be appealable.

Public Registry: There should be a single, national registry of all CSOs that is accessible to the public.

Termination, Dissolution, and Liquidation: A CSO should be permitted to voluntarily terminate itself; termination by the governmental supervisory organization should only happen for the most flagrant of violations; all involuntary terminations should be subject to objective judicial supervision.

Permitted Purposes and Activities: Like other entities, CSOs should be permitted to engage in activities for the benefit of their members and for public benefit or "charitable" activities. As key participants in public policy debates, CSOs should have the right to speak freely about all matters of public significance, including debate about, and criticism of, existing or proposed state policies and actions. Any CSO engaging in an activity (e.g., health care, education) that is subject to licensing or regulation by a state organization should be subject to the same generally applicable licensing and regulatory requirements and procedures that apply to activities of individuals, business organizations, or public organizations.

Qualification for Public Benefit Status: When a separate state organization determines that another organization qualifies for public benefit or charitable status, such an entity should be an independent, mixed commission (with representatives of the public, the government, and the CSOs themselves). [xix]

Media Access: CSOs should have access to media outlets (including state-owned media) to publicize their activities.

Funding: All organizations must be allowed to freely receive all the available licit forms of internal and international cooperation.

Public Action and Advocacy

Public action and advocacy– that is, citizens coming together against repressive measures – may take various forms, such as demonstrations, letter-writing campaigns, public comment, and media campaigns.[xx] Other means of advocacy include cyber-activism (blogs, newsletters, etc.), SMS campaigns, and political lobbying.[xxi]

Domestic Public Action

CSOs have successfully taken public action in various countries by rallying international and expert support, raising awareness of the restrictive provisions among stakeholders, organizing meetings, and attracting the attention of the media. In Peru, such actions succeeded in inducing the government to rescind restrictive provisions of a recently proposed law.[xxii]

Mass mobilization

This can be another effective tool. Organizing large groups of people to demonstrate can be an effective way of protecting civil society. For example, the 2007 Student Movement Campaign in Venezuela was successful it its attempt to mobilize the population, to shake off citizen apathy, increase public demand for solutions to social problems, and raise their voices against the restrictions of the right to freedom of expression. In 2008, civil society movements helped organize public demonstrations in Managua (Nicaragua), opposing Daniel Ortega's authoritarian behavior and violations to the constitution. A million students and teachers in Chile protested for educational reform in 2006.[xxiii] Strikes and boycotts can also be effective.

Global advocacy, lobby and networking

International Diplomacy: Diplomacy can be an effective tool through which leaders of other nations and international institutions can open discussions with a government to dissuade it from pursuing repressive legislation, and offer political maneuvering room for it to change course publicly. Diplomatic persuasion for less restrictive legislation on the part of American Secretary of State Rice resulted in a more liberal legislative regime.[xxiv]

International pressure: Publicly-applied pressure on the part of the international community can be effective in reversing the actions of repressive regimes towards CSOs. International support can also ease feelings of isolation among repressed groups, whose hope may be bolstered by the knowledge that the international community is fighting for their rights.[xxv]

Belong: NGOs in countries like Iran, Venezuela, Nicaragua, among others, have been demonstrating over time the importance of being registered and participating in international and regional organizations. In Peru, during the Fujimori's authoritarian and repressive regime, NGOs were an active factor for change and were involved in several initiatives at the Organization of American States (OAS) and the Inter American Human Right System. The same can be true with the participation of NGOs from countries with authoritarian regimes with the opportunity and protection from the UN (registration at the ECOSOC takes time, but it gives the opportunity to participate and a voice) or from regional organizations. The same opportunities can be had with structured networks of civil society like Civicus[xxvi] or CONGO.

South-South Effective Diplomacy

Government-Government (Bilateral): In terms of how to deal with elected authoritarians, those who persecute opposition and violate democratic values human rights, the best solution is effective South-South diplomacy—for governments like Brazil, who have been successful, to positively engage countries like Venezuela and Nicaragua on issues of human rights and democracy. We need governments that have carved out democratic paths to assist in exporting democracy to this "other" America so that it too can share in the prosperity. , Democratic countries in Latin America have tremendous potential when it comes to sharing democratic stories and lessons with their more authoritarian neighbors, and it is exactly this, as well as holding the feet of leaders in this other Latin America to the fire. Democratic governments in Latin America should align their foreign policy with their expressed domestic commitment to democracy and human rights. Brazil, Chile, Costa Rica, Uruguay and Panama, among others, have been consolidating their democracies internally and have thus increased the opportunities for their civil societies to advance democracy and human rights in other countries.

Civil Society/Government-Government: some democratic countries have seemingly loaned support to the repressive countries. It is important that newly emergent democracies do not forget their global commitment to democracy in the tranquility that has corresponded with their political and economic success. Further action is required to promote an awareness of the status of democracy countries' outside one's own—to more actively engage civil society organizations and diplomats to further democracy across borders, to consolidate democracy in Latin America as a whole rather than leaving the continent to be divided in two, one democratic and successful and the other not. Civil society can put pressure in their own governments to be more responsible at the international level and avoid support to autocrats and support democratic movements in other countries.

Civil Society/Government-Civil Society: Effective diplomacy is possible. For example, look at how the Czech Republic has engaged Cuba, allowing Cuban civil society leaders to use computers in its embassy to blog free from the Castro regime's usual controls and leading efforts to strengthen and inter-link civil society groups. With the support from the Czech Government, Czech and Cuban civil society groups have worked with each other on numerous projects. Democratic countries in Latin America are not without similar examples. For example, look at the effective role Conectas, a small civil society organization in Brazil, has had in promoting responsible diplomacy in the south. There are positive examples of South-South diplomacy. We just need more of them, and we need them to be consistent.

Civil Society-Government: organizations in more democratic countries can be an active force pressuring non democratic governments to stop harassment against civil society organizations and leaders.

Civil Society-Civil Society: Civil society organizations in countries like Brazil, Chile and Uruguay should working in conjunction with civil society groups in Cuba, Venezuela and Nicaragua. These groups should share experience, an effective tool building healthier opposition politics and stronger civil society. However, despite enormous potential for cooperation of civil society groups across borders, we too often witness a lack of solidarity between civil society organizations, most importantly between civil society organizations in countries with authoritarian regimes and those with consolidating democracies. Not only this, but

Civil Society-Regional Bodies organizations from more democratic countries have the opportunity to be more active in regional bodies supporting initiatives and organizations in autocratic countries.

My view of South-South Effective Diplomacy requires responsible governments to facilitate the sharing of best practices among civil society organizations, youth groups and other social, political and economic actors, support the construction of civil society networks, educate civil society leaders on the use of new tools and technologies, promote democratic solidarity across the continent, and promote awareness of what has been accomplished in much of the continent. Countries like Venezuela, Nicaragua, Bolivia, and Ecuador should not be left behind. Instead, they should have their eyes opened to the successes experienced in other countries so that they too may build such democratic foundations. North-South diplomacy has its place, but South-South diplomacy also has an important role to play. The United States is not all-powerful, and it is time for democrats in the region to come to together to strengthen regional and sub-regional bodies, to adopt country-to-country initiatives, to level the playing field between authoritarians and democratic forces in the countries left behind.

Overcome barriers to civil society with CSO Diplomacy

Urge established democracies and international organizations to reaffirm their commitments to democratic governance, rule of law, and respect for human rights, and develop consistent policies based on these principles.

Urge established democracies and international organizations to reaffirm that proposed restrictions on freedom of association are subjected to the rigorous legal analytical test defined in Article 22 of the ICCPR (see Under Scrutiny section) and energetically publicize transgressions, particularly on the part of ICCPR signatories.

Urge democratic governments and international organizations to ensure and increase assistance for civil society organizations.

Organize discussions and hearings in parliaments, congresses, and national assemblies to raise lawmakers' awareness of the issues and principles.

Encourage UN special rapporteurs to incorporate the principles outlined here into their reports and other UN documents.

Put pressure on the Ministries of Foreign Affairs and UN representatives.

Actions for Civil Society Organizations

Facilitate national and regional discussions on this topic.

Insist that proposed restrictions on freedom of association are subjected to the rigorous legal analytical test defined in Article 22 of the ICCPR and energetically pursue transgressions, particularly on the part of ICCPR signatories, through energetic publicity and litigation in appropriate international courts.

Translate the reports into local languages.

Use technologies and "virtual" space to conduct democracy and human rights work and to mobilize support for such work.

Go beyond the traditional NGO circles and begin to include activities and information in other circles like schools, universities, professional groups, consulting groups, among others (expand networks).

Actions Directed to Democracy Assistance Organizations

Encourage democracy assistance foundations to facilitate national, regional, and international discussions among civil society groups to develop ideas for reforming legal frameworks for civil society work.

Insist that proposed restrictions on freedom of association be subjected to the rigorous legal analytical test defined in Article 22 of the ICCPR and energetically pursue transgressions, particularly on the part of ICCPR signatories, through energetic publicity and litigation in appropriate international courts

Ensure that democracy assistance foundations and organizations distribute reports such as the World Movement for Democracy's "Defending Civil Society" report to all of their partners and grantees around the world.

Consensus

Only broad consensus helps to avoid the risk that puts in jeopardy the continuity and stability of social policies or sustainable development initiatives. Those reforms and the changes of paradigms can take a long time. Only broad consensus protects those policies from change in the government. It is also true that only policies developed with strategic planning and long term objectives, and short term urgent actions can produce the kind of results necessary to achieve true democracy.

Strengthen independent institutions and rule of law

According to this research there is a relationship between democracy and development, and between effective government and the health future of any country.

Effective governments must look for economic growth with social priorities

That includes planning, developing social programs, giving priority to a social agenda in the economical and political arena, increasing the weight of social and environmental programs within the national budget and improving the management, efficiency and quality of social programs.

Raising Public Awareness

Civil society and its partners can work to raise international awareness of threats to the right of free association and to harassment of civil society groups.[xxvii] By raising awareness effectively, local groups and coalitions can obtain support from the broader civil society community and from the public, as well as from other nations and international bodies, leading to domestic and international pressure on the government.[xxviii]

Popular Education

Tactics used to reach a broad audience may include the distribution of educational leaflets, brochures, and pamphlets, the distribution of shirts, posters, and stickers, the use of artwork like caricatures, cartoons, sketches, and possibly graffiti to highlight issues, the use of media and the internet, and demonstrations. One innovative form of education is street theatre – plays meant to inform citizens about specific issues. Another is citizen journalism in Venezuela.

Rights-Based Education

Many NGOs engage in activities designed to raise awareness of the human and legal rights guaranteed to individuals living in repressive contexts. Right-based education can range from the distribution of easy-to-read educational material to its integration into university curricula.[xxix]

Training for Civil Society Activists

A more targeted way to raise awareness is to run programs that provide legal training for those working in the civil society sector. Educating civil society practitioners on the legal framework in which they are working can help them operate in the complex and contradictory legal context in which they find themselves.

Monitoring and Documentation

A vital component of raising awareness is communicating to the world exactly how the state is violating the rights to freedom of association and expression and thereby threatening civil society. To do that, CSOs must monitor the situation through research, investigation, documentation, analysis, and reporting. For example, CIVICUS produces a monthly bulletin reporting on the state of civil society rights around the world.[xxx] Similarly, the International Freedom of Expression Exchange (IFEX)[xxxi] runs a network that issues "action alerts" to expose media-freedom violations.[xxxii] *Ratings Mechanisms* are a specific form of monitoring used to measure the compliance of governments with rights-based standards. For example, NGOs and well as various governments[xxxiii] produce regular publications offering comparative studies measuring progress and obstacles to democratization in countries around the world.[xxxiv] Organizations like Freedom House also develop, maintain, and publish good democracy and freedom indexes.

Use of Media

Media – newspapers, radio, television, and the Internet – is a powerful tool for protecting civil society and reducing human rights violations. The use of media can raise awareness, expose violations, and mobilize support. In situations where the media is controlled by a repressive government, it may be helpful to attract the attention of international media.[xxxv] Some organizations in the region have been developing their own media outlets. In Peru, during the Fujimori's autocratic regime, the CSO Instituto de Defensa Legal (IDL) developed a radio network to organize communities, promote human rights and democracy, and challenge government violations.

2.0 Media and Platforms

Training CSO and activist in the effective use of 2.0 and 3.0 technologies to be effective in terms of communications, disseminations of the ideas and activism is one of the fundamental tools for survival in restrictive environments. The use of blogs, twitter, pin and other mechanisms have becoming fundamental tools for communication in Cuba, Venezuela and in the successful revolutions in the Arab world. Better training in the use of this platforms and a coordination of efforts among CSO and leaders can be an incredible resource to empower organizations and develop effective campaigns.

Protective Alliances and Networks

Whether they are formal or informal, national or international, networks promote information sharing and cooperation and may provide hope and protection from violence and oppression to organizations working within restrictive environments. Networks may communicate through meetings, email, or more formal umbrella groups. The benefits of inter-CSO networks include shared resources, an enhanced profile, and a larger base of constituents. Networks enable international information-sharing and can have international leverage.[xxxvi] The Latin American and Caribbean Network for Democracy is a good example.

Direct Support to Victims of Violations

In countries with particularly oppressive regimes, where civil society activists are arrested or imprisoned, providing direct support to the victims can make an important difference. The US has developed a program to help provide direct medical, legal, financial, and emotional support to journalists under pressure in authoritarian countries. This program could be emulated to support civil society workers as well as journalists.[xxxvii] Some proposals to create a special Global Fund for protecting NGOs have been presented at the UN and other international organizations. There are several proposals at the OAS to create a fund to protect human rights activists and journalists.

Going Underground

When civil society organizations face an utter lack of legal space – "whether through denial of registration, termination, suspension of activities, prohibition, harassment, imprisonment, or some other cause"[xxxviii] – it may nevertheless be possible to persevere.[54]

Create a Parallel Structure

When a government decides to go against freedom of association and establish severe restrictions for the operation of NGOs, the best suggestion is to be creative. Cuba's NGOs now work underground or work only as "voluntary groups". International cooperation comes to Cuba in the form of goods and services, and cooperation resources have been channeling through Costa Rica, Mexico, or US partner groups. Sometimes the alternative, when the regime decides to establish limitations on NGOs, is to create a parallel for-profit company and manage the resources with the company and the programs with the NGO. Venezuelan NGOs have been opening accounts in other countries to limit scrutiny from the government. In cases like China, Iran, Cuba, Burma, among others, several NGOs created an international organization based in another country. For international cooperation one of the alternatives is to help with printing materials (outside the country), individual contracts (for the staff) as consultants, payment directly to services and products, among other indirect payments.

Support alternate activities

NGO laws typically regulate the activities of the NGOs and the international cooperation. In some cases the alternative to funding can be indirect support. Some NGOs in this environment organize raffles, concerts, movie premiers, and other fund raising activities. The alternative for international cooperation is to help them with the cost (by direct payments to service providers), or to contribute to cover the cost of the artists involved, for example.

Improve Efficiency, transparency and accountability of the NGOs:[xxxix]

One of the tools is to achieve efficient and transparent NGOs to avoid false excuses for regulation from any regime.[xl]

Integrity and Good Governance: Transparent and honest NGOs can prove that any action from the governments is against freedom of association and reverse any negative campaign from any regime.

---

54 Here are a few examples: Polish Solidarity was established in 1980. As an umbrella group for a range of social and political causes united in their opposition to the communist regime, the organization was soon declared illegal and its leaders were arrested. Nevertheless, Solidarity continued to operate underground for almost a decade.54 Some Venezuelan CSOs have been opening their registration in other countries like Peru or the US so they can keep operating or receiving foreign assistance. Several groups in Cuba operate thanks to their counterparts in Costa Rica or the US. A decision from the DC Court of Appeals allowed US Government or US Funded Foundations not to publish or distribute the names of their grantees from Venezuela to avoid persecution from the Venezuelan government, providing a humanitarian exemption to the Freedom of Information Act.

Financial Sustainability: Improve the conditions necessary for the financial sustainability to prevent the effect of any restriction to international sources and avoid depending on only one source (diverse funding sources).

Accountability and Transparency: NGOs are accountable to their constituencies, to the public, donors, and to the beneficiaries. Some private accountants provide pro-bono services to help NGOs develop their own system and keep the organization transparent.

Reporting Generally: To the maximum feasible extent, all reports required of CSOs should be as simple to complete and as uniform among state organizations as is possible.

Transparency: Some organizations in Latin America created a network for CSOs transparency which helps organizations to have internal and external controls and demonstrate transparency. Some accountant firms have been helping Colombian groups (pro bono) to have a perfect accountability.

International Support: Groups like the International Center for Non Profit Law have been helping organizations from Bolivia, Ecuador, and Nicaragua to fulfill the government regulations and requirements.

Self Regulation

Not-for-profit organizations can adopt high standards of transparency and accountability, and bilateral policy agreements (as distinct from regulatory or legislative measures) with a collective of voluntary sector representatives.[xli] Some NGOs get together to develop codes of conduct or to propose other standards or frameworks. Some NGOs from Colombia have been combining their efforts to develop a common code of conduct and also to establish guidelines for transparency for NGOs. They created a system of publicity for budgets and programs (on-line) of NGOs and audits inside the network. In other cases, transnational NGOs also developed codes of conduct and auditing processes and a certification process.

Regional Level

Some organizations have been promoting changes at the Organization of American States to improve democracy monitoring mechanisms and also to provide a permanent forum for the participation of Civil Society Organizations. Some groups also developed a proposal to create a special unit at the OAS' Human Rights Commission to protect CSOs.

Courage and faith

One of the fundamental tools is to have faith in the work that the NGO performs and keep the courage to keep working and be innovative.

Courage in donors
Courage in activists
Courage in staff, directors, and all the members of the NGOs
Courage in student groups
Courage in the media and journalists to challenge injustice.

Conclusions

Latin America is facing a very difficult time for moving toward democracy; authoritarian and populist leaders have been using elections to get into power and obtain a "legitimate" government. Belligerency grows as bilateral and internal conflicts arise in our international community. In this process we also see fear in the eyes of autocrats or authoritarians at the power of civil society with the obvious result of a backlash for human rights in the Bolivarian Alliance Countries (Alba Countries), in particular freedom of association.

Every regime has its own character. In some cases we can see success in stopping anti-NGO laws, like in Venezuela or Peru, where a positive internal and international campaign, with the help of donors and international organizations forced the regimes to slow down the process of approving new legislation. In the case of Ecuador or Bolivia, NGOs developed innovative strategies to keep working, as did Nicaragua. Now it is almost impossible for a regime to impose restrictions NGOs without paying the price. Two of the elements that convinced the Community of Democracies to exclude the government of Venezuela were its attacks on free media and the proposed legislation against NGOs. With a world moving faster with new technologies it is just a matter of time before the backlash is broken.

The study shows common patterns of conduct among Alba countries and an increase similarity among different measures to limit freedom of association, operation and expression of CSOs and their leaders. This study found terrible environment to operate for CSOs in Cuba, Venezuela and Nicaragua and a clear pattern of limitations and repression in Ecuador and Bolivia.

Innovative approaches, coordination, common goals, and courage can be a solid base for NGOs using the tools for survival of NGOs under threats from the regimes, and even in the case of totalitarian regimes. Experience has shown that national coordination with international support can stop these threats to human rights or be a tool for survival as well.

Some organizations in very repressive environments have been proving that it is possible to fight against very repressive regimes, like the brave organizations in Cuba, China, Venezuela, and Nicaragua, among others. After decades of repression, exile, and terror, the NGO leaders are still there, building democracy and defending human rights. In some cases, activists have been accused of being subversive and unpatriotic, or agents of foreign countries. Some dissidents in Cuba have been taking the decision to promote liberty with their lives, through terminal hunger strikes. The Cuban dissident Ariel Hidalgo (1994) wrote the following illustrative view of social domination:

Where the seeds of civil society exist, the social contradictions represented by legal means will, by necessity, emerge illegally, at the margins. Despite a rigid totalitarian structure, social forces that contest the regime are inevitable, such as parallel trade unions, human rights committees, and independent cultural, religious, and environmental associations. Thus even under totalitarianism, an opposition can arise with the proper preconditions. [xlii]

Even when the international community must help NGOs and improve networks, NGOs and activists cannot rely on the international community or international legislation to improve the conditions in their countries, or to prevent possible backlash in terms of democracy and freedom of association. They need to put more effort and attention in local networks, working at the national and local levels with all the sectors, creating ownership of the "International principles protecting civil society", and educating the public about the role of organizations and activists as fundamental elements of true democracy. It is important to go beyond the traditional NGO models and try to create better networks with universities, social groups, professional associations, schools, local governments, among other sectors.

It is a shared human effort for democracy worldwide and NGOs have been facing challenges through this process for a long time. This backlash will be reversed with networking, innovation, transparency, and courage.

Knowledge makes us realize that we are ignorant and need to continually learn. The more we study any particular situation or any area of human knowledge, the more we realize there is so much more to research. This is just as true when studying Latin America; the more we delve into the subject, the more in-depth study is needed into the causes that are historical; that go beyond any initial approach.

This study begins with the terrible backlash against CSOs in the Alba countries, establishing the direct relationship between governance and sustainable development, and evaluating, the current political and ideological situation of the region. The clear turn of Latin America toward center left is obvious, with the cases of Paraguay, El Salvador, Guatemala, Brazil, Uruguay, and Argentina. Also obvious is the trend toward the radical populists and the authoritarian left of Venezuela, Ecuador, Bolivia, and, Nicaragua and the effects in terms of the restrictions to freedom of association.

The study included a comparative view with other countries in the region and we can appreciate the levels of respect and freedom of association in more democratic countries in the region. The study showed that more democratic the country the best mechanisms for civil society to freely operate.

Now is the time for civil society and political leaders to be effective and change the current negative paradigm in the Alba countries and be innovative to bring democracy and the rule of law to those countries.

Annex I: Common Trends in the Alba Countries

I.   Barriers to Entry

	Bolivia	Cuba	Ecuador	Nicaragua	Venezuela
Limited Rights to Associate and Form NGOs: Some restrictive governments do not grant the right to associate or form organizations.		No legal right to association to democracy and human right groups	NGOs are closely controlled by the government.	The government has been denying some organizations from registration due to their "international connections".	Lack of access to registration, notary services, or incorporation. Restriction to participate in government funded projects
Prohibitions against unregistered groups: Limited registration to certain groups and any activity outside of registration is illegal.		The government does not allow the registration of CSOs and forbids any activity of any group, considering it illegal		Any activity from an unregistered group is illegal and can be prosecuted.	Registration is mandatory for any group that wants to operate in Venezuela.
Restrictions on founders: Placing restrictions on eligible founders or requiring difficult-to- reach minimum thresholds for founders is one way to limit the freedom of association.	Only citizens may serve as founders of associations, thereby denying freedom of association to refugees, migrant workers, and stateless persons.	The government does not allow registration.	The government increasingly confused CSOs (non-profit) with for-profit entities and also established certain limitations that jeopardy CSOs	The activities of the agencies duly registered were deemed inconsistent with the purpose for which they were granted legal status, and violated Laws of Associations.	A decision from the Supreme Court (2002) established that organizations with foreign funding, control, or with integrants from any religious group are illegal.
Inability to register and secure the benefits registration: Registration is necessary for an organization to become, and obtain the rights of, a legal person. Some governments make registration so difficult that some groups are prevented from registering, imposing	The government has actively discouraged the creation of human rights organizations by simply not responding	No registration	The government has been changing and imposing new requisites for registration and also requesting re-registration and fulfillment	Several laws and regulations have been implemented to make it impossible to obtain new registrations or renewals	Even when there is not a limitation for registration, Public Registries tend to reject registration from organizations

barriers to registration such as vague registration procedures; detailed, complex documentation requirements; prohibitively high registration fees; and excessive delays in the registration process.	to registration applications from such groups, sometimes for years		of mandatory administrative requirements.	for CSOs	with human rights or democracy objectives
Vague grounds for denial of registration: A common legal tool is the use of overly broad, vague grounds for denying registration applications; often no appeal mechanism is available.	Registration can be refused if "society does not need its services or if there are other associations that fulfill society's needs in the [same] field of activity"	The state controls any registration of any group and it doesn't' allow any registration of CSOs.	Registration may be denied according to the opinion of the government.	If an organization allegedly "conspires" against the regime, or a political party doesn't fulfill some vague requirements, they can deny or suspend the registration.	There have been several cases of denials of registrations to organizations that work in democracy or human rights or any activity that can be perceived as opposition to the current regime.
Re-registration requirements: Such requirements place a burden on civil society and provide the government with regular opportunities to deny registration.		Not possible the registration	Laws require renovations and re-registration process.		The pending Cooperation Law includes a requirement of re-registration to all the NGOs
Barriers for international organizations: Some countries use legal barriers specifically to target international organizations, seeking to prevent or impede their operation inside the country.	International organizations may set up offices, subject to any conditions and restrictions which the Minister imposes	The regime prohibited international organizations to operate in the country.	At the moment there are no specific barriers, but there is a bill/statute under discussion that would regulate international organizations and international cooperation.		The government and the justice system (controlled by the president) have been persecuting, harassing, and using the court system against organizations with international support, and also expelled from the country representatives from Human Rights Watch

					and from religious groups.

II. Barriers to Operational Activity

	Bolivia	Cuba	Ecuador	Nicaragua	Venezuela
Direct (broadly-worded) prohibitions against spheres of activity	NGOs are restricted from engaging in any human rights activities; governmental approval is required for any political gathering. Bolivia's government requested international donors to stop any funding to CSOs that work in human rights or democracy areas	Activities of CSOs ore not allowed in Cuba. Any activity considered by the regime as counter-revolutionary has been persecuted	There are very vague prohibitions such as CSOs may be liable if they offend public order, which is an undefined legal concept, or if the organization does not comply with regulatory requirements. The government closed an environmental NGO just because it was opposed to a non-environmentally friendly project in the Ecuadorian Amazon area		The government has been limiting areas, activities and funding due to national security and the protection of the "revolution"
Invasive supervisory oversight: The government has the right to intervene in NGO operations, including membership, vetoing members, or introducing members of its own choice. Some governments restrict registered CSO activities	Government controls the activities of organizations by authorizing registration authorities to audit their activities and finances and request any of the organization's documents at any time.	Activities of CSOs ore not allowed in Cuba.	Government controls the activities of organizations by authorizing registration authorities to audit their activities and finances and request any of the organization's documents at any time.	State interference in associational activities is authorized by law; government representatives may attend association meetings and associations are required to obtain permission to undertake most activities	Pressure is on national and international donors to reduce or eliminate support to Venezuelan NGOs.

regularly and continuously; failure to comply with government demands leads to sanctions and penalties					
Harassment from Government Officials: Government officials target opposition and NGOs to impede their activities	Intrusive tax inspections of NGOs and burdensome report requirements. Government actions also created self-censorship	Civil Society Organizations have an obligation to provide any information that may be required by the authorities and facilitate access to government officials to carry out physical checks.	Cuba's government persecute all the activists and the government has been placing them in jail violating their human rights.	The government persecutes and harasses human rights and democracy leaders and organizations. The government and its followers have been attacking women's rights groups, destroying their installations, and prosecuting their leaders.	The Inter-American Human Rights Commission admitted a case that claims that the government created the "Maisanta" list with oppositionists and critics to the regime as a "backlist" to deny jobs, public services, and harass critics.
Criminal Penalties Against Individuals Associated with an Organization: Individuals who are found responsible for certain NGO activities can be held criminally liable and fined or imprisoned, which discourages NGO participation	A human rights campaigner was arrested while meeting with local civil society representatives and was reportedly charged with espionage. Opposition or any activity to promote democracy is paid with jail time	Justice system has been used to persecute political activist and CSO leaders	The executive branch represented by the President attacked all the NGOs that have to do with the protests of the indigenous people against the water law project and threatened to sue them	The courts (controlled by the government) have been opening cases against civil society organization leaders and opposition leaders.	"Suspended" sentences against civil society activists are used to avoid international condemnation for imprisoning activists while simultaneously discouraging them from future activism.
Lack of Independent Institutions, Rule of Law or Access to Remedies Against Restrictions or Attacks		No independence in any institution, all the branches of government are controlled by the			President Chávez controls the five branches of government set out in Venezuela's constitution —

51

		authoritarian regime			executive, legislative, judicial, and the so-called "citizens' power" (which includes the Attorney General and the Accounting Office).
Arbitrary or Discretionary Termination and Dissolution: Some governments use their significant discretion to shut down CSOs and use that discretion to quash opposition groups		The government persecute CSO and political activists	New legislations gave broad power to the government to dissolve any organization, including the OSC when it repeatedly violates the provisions issued by the ministries or agencies of control and regulation.	Civic organizations have been arbitrarily terminated. The government also eliminated the registration of several political groups and parties without any legal procedure	The law permits the termination of an NGO when it is "necessary" or "in the best interests of the public."
Establishment of "Parallel" Organizations: Governments form or control their own CSOs (GONGOs) in order to undermine, discredit, and attract funding away from the legitimate CSO sector	The government sponsored and funded a group of "parallel" organizations to compete with opposition CSOs; some of those groups are funded by the Venezuelan government	The government created parallel unions and NGOs to block other organizations at the United Nations and International Workers organizations	The Government established a Secretariat of Peoples with the rank of Minister, to represent civil society and indigenous peoples, and Afro and local peasants.	The government has established GONGOs with the aim of monitoring the activities of independent CSOs (GONGOs attend conferences and report on the activities of CSOs). The government created the Citizens power as a way of societal control.	The regime has been funded through "Missions" and developed a broad base of parallel-governmental organizations to "balance" NGOs.
Lack of Protection: Governments try to avoid direct harassment against NGOs but it doesn't provide for any protection for democracy or human rights	Threats have been made against NGO leaders without any judicial or governmental follow up or interest	The government persecutes directly.	All the individuals and groups have constitutional rights and access to diverse procedures to defend them	Daniel Ortega's government has been gradually undermining the institutionalization of the National Police, to the point that this body of public	The government controls police and military forces and allows any violence against civil society

			from the arbitrariness of the government authorities. Unfortunately, there is no judicial independence to support the State of Law	defense against crime behaves in an arbitrary manner.	activists or journalists.
activists					

III. **Barriers to Speech and Advocacy:** Limitations upon free speech, public policy engagement, and advocacy can severely limit NGOs' effectiveness.

	Bolivia	Cuba	Ecuador	Nicaragua	Venezuela
Prior restraints and censorship/burdens on publication	The government supervises all the printing materials that need exonerations	All the books or any printed material needs the previous approval by the government			Any documentary, printing material, or information that can be perceived by the regime as dangerous or against the "revolution" can be destroyed and the TV channel, publisher, and newspaper can be fined or their license suspended.
Defamation laws: Laws regarding defamation are used to hinder free speech and protect powerful people from scrutiny.		In Cuba there is no freedom of speech	All the individuals and groups have constitutional rights and access to diverse procedures to defend them from the arbitrariness of the government authorities.	Defamation remains a criminal offence for which suspects can be arrested, and subject to hefty fines or imprisonment.	Laws enacting defamation were passed during 2005-2007 and several journalists have been taken to court or jail.
Use of the Justice System and Institutions		The government use the justice system and repression against civil society and political		The government uses the judicial system to persecute opposition leaders and CSOs (omens groups among others),	Supreme Tribunal (Tribunal Supremo) has been implementing decisions against NGOs

		activists.		and the President has been using illegal decrees to keep his friends in the Supreme Court and other courts in the country	and Civil Society (defining the concept of civil society).
Use of Government Ownership of Media Sources and Government Controlled Media			The government closed TV Amazonas and other radio stations due to their work protecting some indigenous groups.	The government has been taking control of the media and uses the same approach as in Venezuela.	The government uses nationally-controlled media (TV, newspapers and radio stations) to threat and defame NGO leaders. It has not renewed licenses to the private sector and increases their media through confiscations.
Use of Government Power to Mandatory broadcasting of messages	Government power is used to force TV and radio stations to cover ongoing allocutions	All the media is controlled by the government	There is an abuse of the "cadenas nacionales" compulsory President public broadcasting, since any mass media that rejects to join the public program may be punished	Government power is used to force TV and radio stations to cover ongoing allocutions. The governments only use pro-government media to publish public and government funded advertising.	Government power is used to force TV and radio stations to cover ongoing allocutions. The governments only use pro-government media to publish public and government funded advertising.
Legal Restrictions to Independent Media: One of the fundamental tools for CSOs is media outlets.	The inclusion of a norm in the constitution requiring that information and opinions disseminated	No independent media and internet control	According with the new Organic Law of Communication the government will create the "Superintendence of Telecommunicatio	Use of governmental telecommunicatio n bodies to control of the media, censorship, and intimidation	The government approved new legislations with ideological contents to limit and

	by the media "respect the principles of truthfulness and responsibility " could lead to arbitrary restrictions of press freedom if enacted in law.		ns and Media (appointed by the President) and its role will be Monitor, Audit, Intervene and Control (Censor) the Media (Art. 48).		control the media, Chavez's government issued the Radio and Television Social Responsibility Law (content control)
Closure to TV or Radio Stations		Non independent TV or Radio Stations	Ecuador's government has been opening administrative procedures and closing TV and Radio stations	Nicaragua's telecom regulator has been canceling permits from opposition radio stations.	RCTV, 34 Radio Stations closed in July and threaten to close 29 more, TV Guayana
Broad, vague restrictions against advocacy: Ambiguous terms are often used to restrict "political" or "extremist" activities, giving the government substantial discretion to punish those whose statements are deemed improper, which in turn serves to chill free expression.	Any public manifestation must be authorized by the government	Public demonstration s are not allowed and the government represses and persecutes any kind of advocacy.	The Ecuadorian constitution indicates that all information must be truthful against the Inter-American human rights dispositions.	The government continuously creates false claims and develops vague restrictions.	Any public act must be authorized by the government and the government supporters also intimidate and harass all the private demonstration s.
Violence and Intimidation	The government uses its violent supporters to intimidate journalists.	The government has been repressing for five decades	Government supporters sometimes physically attack journalists working for critical outlets.	Direct violence against journalists and media owners was justified by the regime. Kidnapping, extortion, and daily violence are the norm.	The government uses security forces and parallel militia and violent groups to limit public engagement and advocacy. The government also created special lists to

					persecute opposition leaders.
Presidential Attacks	Morales often lambasts the private media for backing the opposition agenda and declared them his "enemies".	Cuba is not a free country and the dictator represses any dissidence.	President Correa, has been an active opponent to civil society leaders, journalists and media owners.	Daniel Ortega's personal war wages against Nicaraguan journalist and television anchor, Carlos Fernando Chamorro, and others.	Chavez uses his controlled media and forced messages in all the media to attack directly some CSO leaders or any one he decides to attack.
Restrictions on freedom of assembly: By making it difficult or even illegal for individuals and groups to gather or meet (i.e., to exercise freedom of assembly), the law directly hinders the ability of NGOs to plan or engage in advocacy activities.	The government uses violent followers to repress and persecute opposition leaders and demonstrators	Any meeting or assembly has been forbidden for more than 5 decades.		The government funds violent groups to intimidate and implement a violent response to any kind of democratic assembly. They have been persecuting and shooting congress leaders and CSOs	Intimidation and hearings by Congress Members and deputies for NGO leaders due to "conspirator" and other false allegations. The government uses its violent groups and police forces to intimidate opposition meetings

IV. **Barriers to Contact and Communication:** These restrictions impede the ability of NGOs to receive and provide information, and to meet and exchange ideas with their civil society counter-parts.

	Bolivia	Cuba	Ecuador	Nicaragua	Venezuela
Barriers to the creation of networks: Existing legal entities may be limited or even prohibited in their freedom to form groups, networks, coalitions, or federations.	The government has simply refused to register umbrella groups	The government doesn't allow to create networks	No barriers yet, but there is a real menace that within the communication law the access to the Internet and social networks may be restricted	The Director and Control Department of the Interior Ministry MIGOB, Gustavo Syria, accused the agencies with legal personality to, "have lent their name for these organisms are not registered to receive funding	The government has been attacking organizations with international affiliations. At the Organization of American State, the United Nations, and other international organizations, the government has

				for a range of activities and amounts millionaires"	been trying to block Civil Society Organizations
Barriers to international contact: Governments prevent and inhibit international contact by controlling exit and entry to the country for nationals and internationals.		There are restrictions to international contact and even Internet control		Government diplomats from Nicaragua began placing some basic restrictions to NGOs with international activities	The government does not renew passports for leaders from CSOs and in one case, retained the passport when the person returned to the country. There are specific controls on organizations that want to participate in international events. The government uses its diplomacy to attack organizations at the United Nations, Organization of American States, and other forums
Access to Information	Morales refused to engage with certain press outlets, on occasion naming specific reporters as enemies	No access to information		Only the Official media (TV/Radio/Newspapers/Communitarian media indentified 100% with the government or its political project) have access to official information. The government denied private media equal access to many official events, even in cases when private media had access to government facilities	Only the Official media (TV/Radio/Newspapers/Communitarian media indentified 100% with the government or its political project) have access to official information. The government denied private media equal access to many official events, even in cases when private media had access to government facilities

57

Self-Censorship		The repressive regime created a terrorized population		Terror and intimidation tactics against journalists and media owners	From the three last TV stations in the hand of private parties, two are controlled indirectly by the government with threats and governmental advertising; those TV stations are Venevision and Televen
Use of Governmental Apparatus to Counter-Inform		The government controls all the activities			Development of thousands of web-pages, community media, "independent" journalists, and other forms of information used to promote the "revolution" and attack opposition (100 million dollar campaign per year).

V. **Barriers to Resources:** Some governments restrict the access of CSOs to foreign funding, ostensibly in order to reduce foreign influence.

	Bolivia	Cuba	Ecuador	Nicaragua	Venezuela
Prohibitions against certain categories of funding	All funding must fulfill the priorities of the Government national plan and canalized by the government. By Presidential Decree the government established the requirement of previous approval from the Ministry of Planning and Development to allow any foreign organization to	Provision to external funding. Support to democracy, environment and human rights movements came underground.			Funding from the US is considered against the revolution and organizations that have received those funds have been persecuted, intimidated, harassed, and subject to criminal procedures for "conspiracy with the empire"

	operate in Bolivia.				
Advance government approval: More commonly, the law allows the receipt of foreign funding, but requires advance governmental approval	The government requires pre-approval of funds and a deposit in favor of the government	Not a free country.	Regulations that impose, among other things, reporting and approval mechanisms that give the government control over donor funds and projects. Foreign aid is heavily taxed		
Routing Funding through the Government	Requires all donor funds to flow through government ministries, allowing NGOs to receive funding only if they develop activities according to governmental plans.	The only entity allowed to receive foreign currency is the government	The NGOs Law project presents some threats in this regard		The government implemented an exchange control mechanism that made illegal any form of foreign money transfer not controlled directly by the government
Use of Taxing/Fiscal Authority		No tax benefits	The government over tax the CSOs	Elimination of tax benefits (Arce Law)	Sanctions and fiscal persecution to media owners, media outlets (Globovision) and also denied tax exceptions to CSOs. The government also opened procedures against CSOs and media outlets
Currency Exchange Control		The government is the only one authorized to have other currencies			Since the government implemented an exchange and currency control in 2004 that only allows currency exchange from local currency to dollars or Euros in

					controlled circumstances, there has been the creation of a black market for dollars.

Annex II: Civil Society regulations comparative chart

CUADRO COMPARATIVO DE REGULACIONES

Regulación	Registro y Barreras de Entrada	Posibilidad de operar y Requisitos Organizaciones Extranjeras	Sistema de Registro y seguimiento	Tiempo de Registro	Limitación de actividades	Restricción del Financiamiento	Restricción a la Comunicación	Requisitos Beneficios Fiscales	Informes y vigilancia del Gobierno / Facultades de Disolución
ARGENTINA Constitución, Código Civil y Ley Nacional de Fundaciones 19.836 y normativas de las Provincias	Las organizaciones deben Registrarse e inscribirse ante la autoridad provincial competente con los requisitos establecidos en cada provincia. Si; existe un registro a nivel nacional, donde se registran las asociaciones civiles y fundaciones, que les permite actuar en todo el país y la acredita para todos los actos como personas jurídicas. También existen registros a nivel provincial y registros a nivel municipal. La normativa es clara y accesible en sitios web, como así también asesoramiento gratuito para quienes necesiten constituir este tipo de organizaciones.	No hay restricciones	Existe el Registro Público de ONGs a través del Centro Nacional de Organizaciones de la Comunidad (CENOC). Hay más 13.545 Organizaciones registradas.	3 a 6 meses	Algunas disposiciones administrativas provinciales exigen un mínimo entre $ 2,500 y $ 3,000 de capital en efectivo o en bienes para el registro. Limitación a las actividades sujetas a exoneración fiscal.	No hay restriccio nes. Los coopera ntes son numeros os y esta informaci ón es sumame nte accesibl e en el sitio web de la RACI (Red Argentin a de Coopera ción Internaci onal).	No hay restriccion es	Se requiere la inscripción en el Registro Provincial (personería Jurídica) y luego inscribirse ante la Administrac ión Federal de Ingresos Públicos (Resolució n General 2681 de AFPI)(2010). Las organizacio nes reciben como beneficio no ingresar el impuesto de ganancias ni ser pasivas de retenciones , no ser pasivas de retenciones del Impuesto al valor Agregado y alícuotas reducidas en impuestos bancarios. Los donantes pueden deducir hasta un 5% de la ganancia neta anual para contribucio nes.	A los diversos niveles dependiend o del registro

61

BOLIVIA									
Constitución (Articulo 21), Código Civil y Reglamento DS No. 22409 que crea el Registro Nacional de ONGs	Acta de fundación ante Prefectos de Departamento (otorga personalidad jurídica)	Deben suscribir un Convenio Marco con el Ministerio de Relaciones Exteriores y Culto para su funcionamiento legal y luego inscribirse en el Registro Único Nacional.	Organizaciones deben registrarse en el Registro Único Nacional de ONGS (Decreto Supremo 22409 de 1990), Ministerio de Planeamiento	3 a 6 meses	No hay limitaciones, fines lícitos	El proyecto de Ley de transparencia y Acceso a la Información Publica incluye en su ámbito de aplicación a "las entidades privadas que reciban fondos o bienes, de cualquier origen, para la consecución de fines de interés público o fines sociales".	Los municipios oficialistas en la región de Pando prohíben a organizaciones con fondos de USAID a trabajar en la zona. El gobierno exigió a USAID a no financiar organizaciones de derechos humanos y democracia y USAID acepto. No hay cultura de la donación privada ni beneficios fiscales para estas. El gobierno financia algunos proyectos de desarrollo.	Tramitación de reconocimiento como entidades exentas. Se exonera de: 1) Impuestos sobre utilidades de empresas, 2) Impuesto a la renta presunta de propietarios de bienes, 3) Impuestos a los inmuebles urbanos, 4) Impuesto sobre la utilidad neta, 5) Impuesto a la propiedad de bienes inmuebles, 6) Gravamen aduanero Consolidado (importaciones), 7) Donaciones exentas de Impuesto al Valor Agregado (IVA)	Sistema de registro sistematiza todos los datos y las organizaciones deben presentar cada 3 años información general de las actividades realizadas, financiamientos recibidos y los proyectos programados para el trienio siguiente. A nivel tributario las organizaciones exentas deben presentar anualmente una declaración jurada, estados financieros y memoria anual de actividades. La disolución es Por estatutos y mediante el Decreto Supremo 26140 (2001) se permite controlar y sancionar ONGs que trabajan en zonas de pueblos indígenas/ campesinas pudiendo extinguirlas. Pueden extinguirse cuando violen orden público y buenas costumbres.

BRASIL									
Código Civil, Decreto No. 6.061 (2007) y el Título del Servicio Público Federal fue creado por la Ley 91 de 1935 para el registro de sin fines de lucro. Decreto N° SNJ 24, 11 de octubre de 2007	El Ministerio de Justicia es el órgano competente para otorgar el título de Utilidad Pública Federal y la calificación como Organización de la Sociedad Civil de Interés Público. Ahora es uno de los requisitos para la concesión del Certificado de Asistencia Social Benéfica Entidad (CEBAS). Las organizaciones que ya tengan el título de Utilidad Pública Federal o calificada como OSCIP pueden recibir donaciones de empresas, deducibles de impuesto sobre la renta.	Las organizaciones internacionales que operan en Brasil se registran como nacional - tienen Cadastro Nacional da Pessoa Jurídica (CNPJ) (Registro Nacional de Personas Jurídicas), y no tiene que presentar sus documentos a la SNJ. Esto es debido a que se controlan como cualquier otra ONG brasileña.	En el marco del Decreto N° SNJ 24, 11 de octubre de 2007 publicado en la Gaceta de 10.15.2007, necesariamente debe registrarse en CNE / MJ del Servicio Público Federal, el entidades clasificadas como Organización de la Sociedad Civil de Interés Público (OSCIP), y las organizaciones autorizadas para operar en Brasil. El procedimiento es electrónico/en línea. Sobre la base de datos del Registro de Empresas - CEMPRE 2005, la investigación muestra que existen hoy en Brasil 338 000 organizaciones sin fines	En línea, inmediato	No hay limitaciones. Sin embargo Nuevo Código limita la formación de nuevas fundaciones, sólo para la asistencia religiosa, moral, cultural. A pesar de la restricción puede ser considerado un revés, las categorías son muy amplias e imprecisas, por lo que una interpretación amplia del texto puede cubrir otros fines que no estén expresamente recogidas en la normativa.	No hay limitaciones	No hay restricciones	Las organizaciones gubernamentales son exoneradas del impuesto sobre la renta, impuestos sobre bienes cuando son dedicados a la actividad, impuestos a las ventas en las actividades que desarrolla, así como de algunos impuestos estadales y municipales. Las donaciones hechas por las empresas para las entidades sin fines de lucro que actúan en beneficio de la comunidad pueden deducirse hasta un límite de dos por ciento del beneficio operativo registrado antes de la deducción de la donación computarizada.	Existe una obligación de rendir cuentas anuales en el sistema electrónico de registro y rendición de cuentas que requiere información de los recursos recibidos (públicos y privados), líneas de acción y actividades desarrolladas, uso de los recursos y actualización de representantes de las organizaciones.

63

CHILE	Constitución, Código Civil (1855), Reglamento sobre Concesión de Personalidad Jurídica (2004) y Ley sobre Asociaciones y Participación Ciudadana en la Gestión Pública (2010). Se regula la inscripción, funcionamiento y disolución	No hay barreras de entrada, registro ante autoridades notariales. La nueva Ley establece un nuevo Registro a cargo del Servicio de Registro Civil e Identificación que facilitará la emisión de certificados de vigencia de las organizaciones.	Las permite y deja operar	Registro ante el Servicio de Registro Civil e Identificación, previo documento notariado con estatutos. Se puede solicitar un Certificado de Vigencia. El Ministerio de la Secretaria General de Gobierno (División de Organizaciones Sociales) responsable de las políticas relativas a la participación ciudadana y sociedad civil.	Dos meses (excepciones de más de un año sin explicación)	No hay limitaciones	Chile es un país estable con lo cual se han retirado los financistas internacionales. El Gobierno está buscando mecanismos de apoyo a las OSC, en tal sentido se ha creado un Fondo de Fortalecimiento de Organizaciones de Interés Público.	Limitación en la propiedad de los medios limita libertad de información	Ley No. 19.885 establece los requisitos mediante donaciones directas o al Fondo Mixto de Apoyo Social. Descuento tributario a los donantes hasta el 5% de su renta liquida. Existe un Fondo de Fortalecimiento de la Sociedad Civil y un Fondo de Fortalecimiento de Organizaciones de Interés Público en el Ministerio de la Secretaria de Gobierno para ayudar a las organizaciones	Informes por solicitud del Ministerio. La disolución solo por estatutos.

64

COLOMBIA									
Constitución de Colombia (libertad de asociación, libertad de información, derecho a donar, etc.), Ley 489 de 1998 requiere el involucramiento de ciudadanos y OSC en la política pública.	No siempre es necesario registrarse dado que los grupos y movimientos sociales también están protegidos por la Constitución. Las que se registran deben elaborar y Notariar sus estatutos y documento de constitución. No se exige patrimonio. Se tramita el reconocimiento (es automático no se reconoce) ante las cámaras de Comercio del País con la presentación de estatutos y llenar un formulario. La cámara otorga un Número de Identificación Tributaria NIT provisional.	Algunas alcaldías y gobernacio nes han establecido sistemas de Registro. La Alcaldía de Bogotá estableció el Sistema de Inspección de Personas Jurídicas (SIPJ) para unificar el registro, inspección y vigilancia.	Se les da a las goberna ciones y alcaldía s las facultad es de inspecci ón y vigilanci a. A nivel fiscal se realiza la Direcció n de Impuest os y Aduana (para el IVA y Renta)	24 horas para aprobació n y 3 días para el NIT definitivo y Certificad o de Existencia	Se han dado casos del ataque del Gobierno (en particular el gobierno anterior) contra organizaciones de derechos humanos. Hay restricciones para el uso de fondos públicos.	No hay limitacio nes. Hay requisit os que impone n los bancos para evidenc iar la proveni encia de los fondos para prevenir el lavado de dólares.	Riesgos por grupos ilegales que persigue n ONGs, líderes sindicale s y periodist as	Se da una tarifa menos o la exoneraci ón del Impuesto sobre la renta, pago de IVA solo en actividade s de mercadeo y comercio. Si tienen impuesto municipal es, aranceles de importació n y requisitos laborales. A nivel de donacione s se permite deducir hasta un 30% e la renta liquida de los contribuye ntes para donacione s.	Se deben presentar los estados financiero s dentro de los tres primeros meses del año. Informes tributarios mensuale s

65

COSTA RICA	Ley de Asociaciones (No. 218 de 8 de agosto de 1939) y una Ley de Fundaciones (No. 5338 del 28 de agosto de 1973);	Registro Nacional, Dirección de Personas Jurídicas. La inscripción es necesaria para operar oficialmente y tener la cédula jurídica necesaria para realizar alianzas, vínculos y abrir por ejemplo una cuenta bancaria o una línea telefónica	El proceso de registro es complicado, se deben registrar como organizaciones nacionales. Exceso de leyes, trámites y permisos para inscribir una Organización o una filial en el país. Costa Rica es casi el único país en el continente en no suscribir la Convención de Apostilla, por este motivo y el exceso de leyes (que parece ser una tradición en el país) es dificultoso, engorroso, costoso y excesivamente lento el trámite y aprobación de inscripción de organizaciones y/o filiales en el país.	Se deben registrar ante el Ministerio de Gobernación (Fundaciones) y las demás ONGs ante el Registro Civil Municipal. Luego se requiere el registro y presentar informes al SAT.	Por ley deberían ser 10 días hábiles pero en la práctica es un procedimiento burocrático o que lleva entre 6 meses y 2 años	En el caso de las Organizaciones u Asociaciones es necesario incorporar a un funcionario público en la directiva así como los estatutos de la organización inscritos correctamente. En el caso de filiales es más complicado porque implica poderes oficializados por la gobernación del estado o ciudad donde esté constituida la organización en su sede central. Los funcionarios de registro tienen todo el poder de pedir nuevos requisitos y aprobar o rechazar a libre criterio. Cancillería, abogados y notarios públicos. documentos sean aprobados sino que normalmente se piden más requisitos	No hay	No hay	Las Asociaciones y Sociedades Anónimas están exentas de impuestos en el país	Se requieren Se solicita un breve informe contable anual. En Costa Rica la ley sanciona con multas a los funcionarios de una asociación que no mantengan los libros al día. La no presentación de informes obligatorios puede dar pie a la imposición de multas e inclusive a la cancelación de la personalidad jurídica

CUBA	Ley 54/85-Ley de Asociaciones y su Reglamento, que establece los requisitos para su creación, registro y funcionamiento	La solicitud de autorización para la constitución de una asociación se hará por sus fundadores o iniciadores ante el órgano, organismo o dependencia estatal que tenga relación con los objetivos y las actividades que desarrollará la asociación que se pretende constituir. Si es tratare de una asociación de carácter provincial o municipal, la solicitud se presentará ante el Comité Ejecutivo de la Asamblea del Poder Popular de la provincia o municipio que corresponde. El órgano, organismo o dependencia estatal que reciba la solicitud emitirá, dentro de los noventa días siguientes, un informe al Ministerio de Justicia en el que exponga si procede la constitución de la asociación de que se trata, teniendo en cuenta la correspondencia de los objetivos de ésta con los fines de las actividades que aquéllos desarrollan. El Ministerio de Justicia dictará la resolución correspondiente dentro del término de sesenta días a partir de la fecha en que reciba el informe autorizando o denegando la constitución de la asociación.	No pueden operar	Controladas por el gobierno. En el Ministerio de Justicia tiene un Registro de Asociaciones Nacionales y en cada provincia y en el Municipio Especial Isla de la Juventud, existe un Registro de Asociaciones adscripto a las correspondientes direcciones de Justicia de los órganos del Poder Popular, donde deben inscribirse las asociaciones constituidas en sus respectivos territorios. La inscripción de las asociaciones en el registro que corresponda determina a su personalidad jurídica.	150 días para autorizar o rechazar. No son aprobadas cuando "cuando sus actividades pudieran resulta lesivas al interés social	Las asociaciones deben tener un número mínimo de 30 miembros, sus actividades no deben resultar lesivas al bienestar público o al de otros individuos y entidades privadas, deben respetar el orden constitucional y la legalidad y "No oponerse a los principios de humanismo, independentismo, solidaridad, no discriminación, equidad y justicia social que rigen a la sociedad cubana"	No pueden recibir financiamiento	No hay libertad de expresión	No hay sistema fiscal	Los órganos, organismos o dependencias estatales cuidarán que las asociaciones con las cuales mantienen relaciones utilicen los recursos de ésta en beneficio social y en cumplimiento de la finalidad y objetivo que determinaron su constitución. Los registros de asociaciones ejercerán las funciones de control, supervisión e inspección de las asociaciones. El gobierno puede sancionar o cerrar libremente a las asociaciones.

ECUADOR										
Constitución, Código Civil (1861), Reglamento para la Aprobación de Estatutos, Reformas y Codificaciones, Liquidación y Disolución y Registro de Socios y Directivas de Organizaciones Previstas en el Código Civil y en las Leyes Especiales (El Reglamento) (reformado mediante Decreto Ejecutivo No. 982 del 2008)	Código Civil establece que el otorgamiento de personalidad jurídica corresponde al Presidente de la Republica que delega en el Ministerio de la actividad y estos acordaron unificar criterios mediante el Ministerio de Coordinación de Desarrollo Social. Se debe presentar el acta de asamblea y los estatutos al Secretario General de la Administración Pública y al Sistema de Registro Único de las Organizaciones de la Sociedad Civil (manejado por la Secretaria Nacional de Pueblos, Movimientos Sociales y Participación Ciudadana) (www.sociedad civil.gov.ec). Pueden operar grupos no registrados pero con derechos limitados fiscales. Requiere de $400 patrimonio para el registro.	Requieren del Registro en el Ministerio de Relaciones Exteriores, Comercio e Integración y requieren de un Convenio para su funcionamiento. El Decreto Ejecutivo No. 699 de 2007 crea el Sistema Ecuatoriano de Cooperación Internacional que busca que los proyectos con cooperación internacional se adecuen a los planes del gobierno de Ecuador	Mediante el Sistema de Registro Único de las Organizaciones de la Sociedad Civil por vía electrónica. Se estima el número de asociaciones y organizaciones en más de 45,722. Las ONGs participan del Concejo Ciudadano de Participación y Control Social para la postulación de autoridades públicas.	El Ministerio del Ramo tiene 15 días luego de presentados los documentos, da 5 días para completar cualquier documento faltante del interesado y en ese caso en otros 15 ya aprobar o negar.	No existen limitaciones a las actividades, sin embargo el gobierno tiene amplias facultades de control/discrecionalidad y por ley no pueden tener gastos administrativos superiores al 10% de los ingresos.	Amplias facultades de control y cierre por parte del gobierno (ha cerrado organizaciones arbitrariamente), persecución, etc. El sistema de Registro incluye información delicada de miembros, transito de los mismos, fondos, etc. Los costos de registro hacen imposible para personas de pocos recursos el registro de organizaciones. La nueva Ley propuesta por el gobierno permite el cierre de una organización si no provee información en menos de 15 días.	Pese a no haber limitaciones, las ONGs de derechos humanos y democracia han sido duramente atacadas por el gobierno. El gobierno viene usando el Poder Judicial y restricciones establecidas en el Código Penal para restringir la protesta pública y perseguir manifestantes y personas.	Organizaciones registradas pueden solicitar exoneración del Impuesto sobre la Renta, ese monto es considerado una "subvención de Carácter Público". Se exime de los Impuestos de Aduana cuando son servicios de salubridad, alimentación, asistencia médica, educación investigación científica y cultural cuando tengan contratos con el gobierno. No hay normativa que de beneficios, créditos o beneficios fiscales a donantes lo cual desmotiva para las donaciones en el Ecuador.	Los ministerios pueden requerir cualquier información, de igual forma se deben llenar la información en el Sistema de Registro (que es publica y en línea), informes laborales, informes fiscales y aquellas que reciban más de $100,000 deben llenar un informe anual específico. El Decreto Ejecutivo No. 982 introduce en el 2008 requisitos, controles y causales de disolución que dan excesiva discrecionalidad del Estado para controlar y disolver organizaciones

EL SALVADOR	Constitución, Ley de Asociaciones y Fundaciones sin Fines de Lucro (LAFSFL) (1996) y su Reglamento y Código Municipal (Asociaciones Comunales). Se regula la creación, funcionamiento y disolución	Se formaliza por escritura pública (notario público) y se rige por estatutos internos. Se presenta luego el documento a la Dirección General de Registro del Ministerio de Gobernación (90 días para revisar y 45 días tiene el interesado para enmiendas de observaciones). Ministerio de Gobernación emite un Acuerdo Ejecutivo que reconoce la personalidad jurídica y ordena su inscripción en 60 días hábiles (luego de eso es automática)	Iguales beneficios. Requiere estar debidamente constituida en su país de origen, abrir residencia en el país y mantener en El Salvador un representante con facultades amplias	Registro de Asociaciones y Fundaciones del Ministerio de Gobernación (RAF)		No limitaciones. Cualquier objeto lícito, sin fines de lucro y apolítica. La Dirección General de Registro ha solicitado información no establecida en la Ley. Mucha discrecionalidad. Altos costos de registro (Entre $ 250 a $ 1000)	No hay restricciones	No hay restricciones	Requiere de calificación de la Dirección General de Impuestos Internos del Ministerio de Hacienda (utilidad pública). Otorgada por un año renovable, automáticamente extendida salvo notificación contraria. Requiere presentación de informes, reportes e información tributaria. Exentas de impuesto sobre la renta.	Información periódica al RAF y al Ministerio de Hacienda. Informes mensuales de donaciones recibidas (para mantener sin fines de lucro). Disolución por estatutos y forzada si realiza actividades ilícitas

69

GUATEMALA										
Constitución, Código Civil y Acuerdos Gubernativos, AG 515-93. Se regula la creación, funcionamiento y disolución	El Acuerdo Gubernativo 649-2006 crea el Sistema Único del Registro de Personas Jurídicas del Ministerio de Gobernación (SIRPEJU) y le asigna la responsabilidad de inscribir a las asociaciones civiles. Se exige un mínimo de 7 personas individuales o jurídicas capaces y 80% de nacionales. Una vez inscrita en el M.G. se elabora el acta notarial. Desde el 2009 se llevan controles excesivos hacia organizaciones nuevas con limitaciones a sus estatutos, juntas directivas y otras intervenciones del Ministerio de Gobierno, dificultando el registro a "asociaciones que no están a su gusto". Las organizaciones están obligadas a registrarse en el SAT y luego en la Contraloría General de Cuentas.	El Código Civil exige que estén constituidas y autorizadas según las leyes del país de origen. Sin embargo para organizaciones nacionales solo se permite que el 25% de sus miembros fundadores sea extranjero.	Se deben registrar ante el Ministerio de Gobernación (Fundaciones) y las demás ONGs ante en Registro Civil Municipal. Luego se requiere el registro y presentar informes al SAT.	entre 10 y 45 días hábiles	No hay limitaciones siempre que sean lícitos y no contrarios a la ley. Hay una represión tradicional continua contra las ONGs. Políticos, funcionarios públicos, diputados y grupos de interés han creado muchas ONGs para enriquecerse, depredando el presupuesto y desprestigiando al sector de las ONGs	No hay restricciones	No hay restricciones	Una vez inscritas las OSC deben inscribirse en la Superintendencia de Administración Tributaria (SAT) en un plazo de 30 días hábiles so pena de multas. Exentas del pago de diversos impuestos, impuesto sobre la renta y actividades, aduanas, solo se paga el impuesto al Valor Agregado por las compras. Se debe llenar un formulario de verificación de fondos por inversiones extranjeras. Los donantes pueden descontar de sus impuestos las donaciones otorgadas a OSC.	Las ONGs no son objeto de acoso por parte del gobierno, ni de inspecciones frecuentes ni amenazas. Fundaciones, asociaciones de interés público están sometidas a la vigilancia del Estado y pueden ser intervenidas por el ejecutivo "cuando el interés público lo requiera". El Acuerdo Gubernativo 515-93 asigna al Ministerio de Gobierno "la inspección y vigilancia" de las organizaciones para verificar el cumplimiento de las leyes y de sus normas estatutarias. Las casi 300 ONGs que manejan fondos del Estado son también fiscalizadas por la Contraloría General de Cuentas, además de la fiscalización de la prensa y otras ONGs

| HONDURAS | Constitución Nacional (libertad de Asociación), Código Civil y Ley Especial de Fomento para las Organizaciones No Gubernamentales de Desarrollo (ONGD)(aprobada en abril 2011) Decreto No. 32-2011. Reglamento (no elaborado) | Registro ante la Secretaria de Gobernación y Justicia. Se constituye en asamblea y escritura pública y luego se debe solicitar ante el Poder Ejecutivo su personalidad jurídica, por medio de la Secretaría de Estado en los Despachos de Interior y Población. Aproximadamente 9865 ONGs. La nueva Ley de sociedad civil establece que solo se le puede negar el registro a una organización si fallan en cumplir las mejores prácticas internacionales. | Las ONGD internacionales que deseen iniciar operaciones en Honduras podrán hacerlo a través de una oficina de representación, en actividades similares a las autorizadas en su país de origen, solicitando el reconocimiento o de su personalidad jurídica ante la Secretaria del Interior y Población | Se crea por la nueva ley el Registro de las ONG donde tendrán que rendir cuentas de sus actividades y presupuestos. Y la Superintendencia de las ONG para efectos de regular la creación y el funcionamiento de las Organizaciones, adscrito a la Secretaría de Gobernación y Justicia, a cargo de un superintendente y dos adjuntos quienes serán nombrados por el Congreso Nacional por un período de cuatro años. Se crea oficina especial de enlace para identificar todas las ONG que existen en el país a través de la Secretaría del Interior, con el fin de determinar cuáles rinden informes periódicos y cuáles deben ser canceladas inmediatamente | 3 meses | La nueva Ley También se han endurecido los requisitos para constituir las ONG que con siete miembros se puede fundar, de los cuales una cuarta parte tiene que residir en el país y prohíbe que familiares puedan manejar una ONG, al ordenar que los cuerpos directivos estén integrados al menos por siete personas que no sean parientes hasta en el cuarto grado de consanguinidad. Se puede negar el reconocimiento de la persona jurídica "Si los estatutos y/o reglamentos sean contrarios a los intereses del Estado o atenten contra la moral o el orden público de acuerdo a los tratados y convenciones" internacionales | No hay limitaciones | No hay limitaciones | Los beneficios fiscales están limitados y solo operan en casos de organizaciones que llevan adelante proyectos de beneficencia social reconocidas por el gobierno como elegibles y además bajo amplia discrecionalidad del Director Ejecutivo de la autoridad fiscal. | Registros e informes anuales y la nueva ley establece nuevos registros. Amplias facultades en el gobierno para el control y cierre de ONGs. Tribunal Superior de Cuentas (TSC) debe auditar a todas las organizaciones, tanto nacionales como internacionales, que reciben fondos del gobierno. Pleno poder de control y cierre por parte del gobierno. Se puede sancionar a directivos y miembros también. La Secretaría del Interior y Población ha procedido a cancelar la personería jurídica a más de cien organizaciones inscritas como ONG alegando que se dedicaban a otras actividades. Los fondos que cualquier entidad del Estado destine a una ONGD, serán fiscalizados por la Secretaria del Estado Interior y Población, sin perjuicio de la facultad del Tribunal Superior de Cuentas para verificar que fueron aplicados en la finalidad para la que fueron otorgados |

71

MEXICO	Constitución (Libertad de Asociación), Código Civil y Ley Federal para la Promoción de las Actividades de la Sociedad Civil (2004).	El Registro es a través del Registro Público de Propiedad y en el Registro Federal de Fiscalización. En teoría si hay claridad en el registro, pero los funcionarios de los distintos niveles cuentan con un alto grado de discrecionalidad para interpretar los requisitos que se solicitan. El gran cuello de botella persiste en el cumplir con todos los requisitos que se piden, el segundo, en el tipo de funcionario, de la secretaría de gobernación, que evalúe el expediente, y de su aprobación final	Las organizaciones de la sociedad civil que constituyan los capítulos nacionales de organizaciones internacionales que cumplan con lo establecido en el artículo 3, podrán gozar de los derechos que la misma establece, siempre que sus órganos de administración y representación estén integrados mayoritariamente por ciudadanos mexicanos.	Gran parte de Asociaciones Civiles deben de registrarse ante la Secretaría de Gobernación. Para poder acceder a fondos públicos las organizaciones se deben registrar ante el Registro de Organizaciones de la Sociedad Civil (CLUNI)	Entre 1 a 3 meses	En el caso de las ONGs, OSC, el asesoramiento de un abogado resulta fundamental para poder superar los distintos obstáculos que se le ponen en el registro. Para algunas organizaciones la ley da un control que permite al gobierno de diversas maneras meterse a los asuntos internos de la Sociedad.	No hay restricciones	No hay limitaciones	Sí, hay posibilidad. Aunque muchas veces no es total, hay ONG que hacen eventos altruistas para disminuir impuestos, dado que el apoyo de acciones altruista sirven para deducción de impuestos. Aunque a veces esto ha sido utilizado por los grandes consorcios como Televisa y Tv azteca, pales televisoras, rin que tiene ongs, para disminuir impuestos que deberían pagar.	No existe el Requisito: La petición de informe contable se solicito hace como dos años, pero al momento no se ha aprobado formalmente, aunque algunas organizaciones dicen que tienen que presentar informes anuales a la Secretaria de Hacienda.

NICARAGUA	Constitución Nacional (Art. 49) (Derecho de Asociación). Ley No. 147: "Ley General sobre Personas sin Fines de Lucro" (1992) que regula la creación, autorización, registro y funcionamiento de las organizaciones civiles y religiosas sin fines de lucro. Otras regulaciones aparecen en el Código Civil de 1904. Ley No. 475: Ley de la Participación Ciudadana (2003)	La Ley No. 147 no establece criterios claros de registro (mucha discreción de las autoridades). Es el Congreso Nacional quien le da estatus legal a las OSC (publicado en Gaceta nacional) mediante decreto y estas luego deben registrarse en el Ministerio de Gobierno (Registro y Control de Asociaciones) quien las autoriza para operar. El gobierno ha tratado de implementar un Manual para regular las actividades de las OSC: "Procedimientos de una ventanilla única para la atención a las Asociaciones y Fundaciones Internacionales y Extrajeras sin fines de lucro" del Ministerio de Gobernación y Ministerio de Relaciones Exteriores (en estudio) está diseñado para controlar políticamente a las OSC y limitar su acceso a fondos internacionales.	Las organizacio nes Extranjeras deben Registrarse ante el Departame nto de Registro y Control del Ministerio de Gobierno donde se verifica que estén legalmente constituidas en sus países y sus objetivos cumplan con la Ley No. 147. Existe también un Sistema de Información sobre Cooperació n No Gubername ntal (SysONG) en el Ministerio de Relaciones Exteriores.	Existe el Departamento de Registro y Control de Asociaciones en el Ministerio de Gobierno. Más de 3293 organizaciones registradas	45 días hábiles	No existen limitaciones legales pero el gobierno ha venido intimidando y persiguiendo organizaciones de derechos de mujeres (Ej. Cinco), y otras organizaciones de derechos humanos. Las OSC en Nicaragua han sido perseguidas en diversos gobiernos de Centro de Derecha y de supuesta izquierda, en el gobierno de Arnoldo Alemán las persiguieron por supuestamente ser ligadas al FSLN y ahora por supuestamente "defender los intereses de oposición". Se han tratado desde 1997 diversas leyes y manuales para limitarlas.	No existen limitaciones	El gobierno ha venido atacando directamente y a través de grupos violentos a líderes y organizaciones de derechos humanos	La Ley 453: Ley de Equidad Fiscal y otras leyes dan a las organizaciones de la sociedad civil registrada s y activas excepción de pago de impuesto sobre la renta y del Impuesto al Valor Agregado (IVA) y exoneración de impuestos municipales (Impuesto Sobre Bienes Inmuebles) en los bienes necesarios para el desarrollo de sus actividades.	Las organizaciones deben presentar al final de cada año información de actividades y balance fiscal. Ministerio de Gobierno tiene facultades sancionatorias y de cierre

73

PANAMA										
Constitución de Panamá reconoce la Libertad de Asociación y derecho de reconocimiento de la personalidad jurídica de las asociaciones, Código Civil, Ley 33 (2010), Decreto Ejecutivo 170 (1993) y Decreto Ejecutivo 534 (2005) (crea sistema de registro)	De acuerdo con el Decreto Ejecutivo 524 se crea un Registro de Entidades sin fines de lucro en el Ministerio de Gobierno. Corresponde al Ministerio de Gobierno conceder la personería jurídica y fiscalizar el funcionamiento, junto con la Contraloría General de la república y la Dirección General de ingresos del Ministerio de Economía y Finanzas. Se requiere que tengan fines estrictamente sociales en su acta fundacional, que se afilien a la Ciudad del saber. El Ministerio de Gobierno expide el resuelto para la acreditación ante el Ministerio de Desarrollo Social y la autorización para recibir donaciones deducibles de impuestos. Las organizaciones deben tener un mínimo de 5 miembros todos panameños	Se requiere autorización de quien dirija la entidad en el extranjero, documentación autenticada, escrito que designe representante legal en Panamá, traducción autorizada de la documentación, lista de miembros de junta directiva, poder y carta de solicitud. El Ministerio de Gobierno se encarga del Registro.	Ley 33 (2010) (obligación de organizaciones sin fines de crear un portal de internet donde se publique los donantes). También deben inscribirse en el Registro Único de Contribuyentes (RUC)	6 meses	Existe una restricción para registrar organizaciones "contrarias a las buenas costumbres" y se han dado casos de rechazo del registro a organizaciones que defienden la diversidad sexual. 90% de los panameños no participa de organizaciones gremiales, sociales o sindicales. Solo 700 organizaciones en el Registro. Existe el requisito de un mínimo de 25 miembros.	No hay limitaciones	No hay limitaciones. Se permite competir por fondos del gobierno	Las Asociaciones sin fines de lucro no están en la obligación de presentar Declaraciones de Rentas por los Ingresos que perciben, siempre y cuando dichas rentas o ingresos se obtengan por razón de las actividades para las cuales fueron creadas, pero deben presentar un detalle anual de las donaciones recibidas.	Informe de donaciones vía electrónica con nombre de donantes cubriendo un periodo de 1 año. Llevar el registro de fondos que reciban, generen o transfieran y presentar un informe consolidado al Ministerio de Economía y Finanzas (multas de 50 a 250$ por incumplimiento). Desde el año 2010 deben presentar informes mensuales técnicos y financieros si manejan fondos de "interés público" y mantener la información necesaria para la fiscalización. Mantener por internet toda la información. Disolución por estatutos, pero el gobierno tiene facultad de disolución cuando realicen actividades ilícitas, contrarias a los objetivos descritos en los estatutos, inactividad superior a 5 años, no haber sido inscritas en el registro. Se les multa o revoca la autorización para recibir fondos deducibles de impuesto si presentan información fraudulenta en se retardan en la presentación de informes (Multas entre $ 1,000 y $

74

PARAGUAY	Constitución de Paraguay y Código Civil	Se puede operar sin Registro pero no se da personería jurídica y limitan sus actividades y beneficios. Pera el Registro y la obtención de personería jurídica se hace a través de la Dirección General de Registros Públicos (Poder Judicial)	No hay limitaciones	No existe un sistema de registro coordinado		Poca claridad en el marco tributario, concentración del registro en la capital, lentitud del sistema de registro, dificultad de acceso a la información.	No hay limitaciones. Plena libertad amplios beneficios	No hay Limitaciones	Organizaciones están Exentas del Impuesto a la Renta de Actividades Comerciales, Industriales y de Servicios (IRACIS) y del Impuesto al Valor Agregado (IVA). Las donaciones efectuadas a estas organizaciones son deducibles del Impuesto a la Renta de Servicios de Carácter Personal (IRP) y el IRACIS de individuos o empresas donantes hasta un monto que no supere el 1% del ingreso bruto en el caso del IRP y en el IRACIS el 10% de la renta neta gravada.	Informes requeridos por la Administración Tributaria sobre donaciones, rendiciones de cuenta anual y para prevenir el lavado de dinero. Disolución solo por resolución de su propia Asamblea o por el Poder Ejecutivo si transgreden las leyes

75

| PERU | Constitución y Código Civil. Reglamento de Inscripciones de Registro de Personas Jurídicas No Societarias (Resolución de la Superintendencia Nacional de Registros Públicos). El SUNARP ha dictado el Reglamento de Inscripciones del Registro de Personas Jurídicas No Societarias en Abril de 2009. | Las organizaciones pueden registrarse o no, siendo sujetos de derecho sin registro pero sin autonomía patrimonial. Existe el Registro de Organizaciones No Gubernamentales de Desarrollo (ONGD) nacionales receptoras de Cooperación técnica Internacional (Decreto Legislativo No. 719 y su Reglamento) y la Ley de Creación de APCI (Agencia Peruana de Cooperación Internacional) (Ley 27692). Para la constitución se requiere llevar el acta constitutiva a un Notario Público y luego proceder a una inscripción registral en un Registro Público. El APCI tiene como funciones la conducción y el registro administrativo de Organizaciones No Gubernamentales de Desarrollo (ONGD) Nacionales receptoras de cooperación técnica internacional, de instituciones internacionales de cooperación y | No hay regulación especial para organizaciones extranjeras, se deben registrar en el Registro Publico con sus documentos legalizados y representante legal en el Perú. Hay una sección especial en el Registro Público para entidades extranjeras. | | El plazo de inscripción es de 35 días hábiles prorrogable, puede el Registrador enviar observaciones y se puede acudir a la vía judicial. | No hay limitaciones en las actividades | Los requisitos fiscales y de rendición son tan grandes que se requieren profesionales en las organizaciones que hagan seguimiento a los mismos. Existe la obligación de registro el APCI para organizaciones que reciben cooperación internacional, limitando la libertad de asociación y contratación, así como obligando a un control adicional. Sin embargo por interpretación del Tribunal Constitucional se señala que las organizaciones que quieran | | Existe la exoneración del impuesto sobre la renta y del Impuesto General a las Ventas (IGV). En el caso del IGV que se paga por compras para proyectos financiadas con cooperación técnica internacional se paga previamente y luego se devuelve. Hay una iniciativa grave en estudio que solo devolvería los fondos a organizaciones que no contradigan los objetivos del gobierno. Para la exoneración del impuesto sobre la renta existen restricciones en base a la calificación de lo que son las actividades de la organización para la obtención de la misma, solo aplica | Requisito de Registro ante el APIC, presentación de informes mensuales juradas y anuales del impuesto sobre la renta, llevar registros laborales de empleador y en el caso de Fundaciones las cuentas y balances son sometidas a la aprobación del Consejo de Supervigilancia de Fundaciones. Las entidades de cooperación técnica internacional deben además presentar el plan anual de actividades para el año de inicio. El estado puede imponer sanciones administrativas (multas) por incumplimiento de obligaciones formales (informes, laborales, etc.) y sustantivas (pagos |

		de organizaciones privadas sin fines de lucro receptoras de cooperación internacional de carácter asistencial o educativo.					tener acceso a la devolución del IGV deben inscribirse, las que pueden no inscribirse.		para organizaciones de beneficencia, asistencia social, educación, cultural, científica, artística, literaria, deportiva, política, gremiales y de vivienda. Si no cumple con estas categorías deben cancelar 30% sobre la renta. La crisis financiera ha venido afectando al sector de la sociedad civil.	impuestos, etc.). También hay sanciones por la no inscripción en el APCI o no presentar el Plan Anual. Por último había la facultad de la cancelación del registro y sanciones a directivos que se declaro inconstitucional. También están sujetas a la fiscalización de la Administración Tributaria (SUNAT) y la Autoridad Administrativa del Ministerio del Trabajo. Existe un incentivo de deducible de impuesto sobre la renta para donantes empresariales que no puede exceder del 10% de la renta neta.

| REPUBLICA DOMINICANA | Ley 122-05 Sobre Fomento y Regulación de las Asociaciones Sin Fines de Lucro | Para la obtención del registro de la incorporación de una asociación sin fines de lucro deberá someterse a la Procuraduría General de la República para el departamento judicial de Santo Domingo, o a la Procuraduría General de la Corte de Apelación del departamento correspondiente, mediante solicitud formulada por el o la presidente(a) de dicha asociación | No hay limitaciones simplemente traducir y legalizar los documentos y registrarlos en la Procuraduría. | Los(as) procuradores(as) generales de las cortes de apelación deberán remitir a la Procuraduría General de la República copia de los registros de incorporación de las asociaciones sin fines de lucro incorporadas en cada departamento judicial. La Procuraduría General de la República deberá llevar un registro nacional de todas las asociaciones sin fines de lucro existentes en el país. | Entre 1 mes y 3 meses. Si en 60 días hábiles la Procuraduría no da respuesta a la solicitud de registro la organización queda automáticamente registrada. | No hay limitaciones | No hay limitaciones | No. Pero hay problemas con los proyectos multilaterales y bilaterales que tienen que ser ejecutado vía los Ministerios según el tema. Esa es una limitación que disminuye las posibilidades de un ejercicio independiente del gobierno de turno. También deben ser "habilitadas" las organizaciones que quieran trabajar con fondos públicos o necesiten de autorizaciones del gobierno para acceder a fondos de cooperación. | la ley permite la exoneración y la Ley 11-92 que permite a las empresas deducir de sus impuestos hasta un 5% de la Renta Neta Imponible. | Informes anuales y llevar libros y documentos. La autoridad de Control es la Procuraduría General de la Republica. Informes anuales. Existe también el Centro Nacional de Fomento y Promoción de las Asociaciones sin Fines de Lucro estará adscrito al Secretariado Técnico de la Presidencia, y coordinado a través de la Oficina Nacional de Planificación (ONAPLAN), que funge. como Secretaría Ejecutiva |

78

URUGUAY	Ley N° 15.089 (Policía administrativa de las asociaciones civiles y fundaciones)(1980), Ley N° 17.163, Ley de Fundaciones (1999)	Quién determina la autorización de una Sociedad Civil es el Ministerio de Educación y Cultura (a través de la Ley). Debe existir una asamblea constitutiva en su fundación y tener reuniones periódicas. No hay limitaciones de miembros máxima pero debe contar con un mínimo de 14 integrantes. Elecciones periódicas de las autoridades (cada dos o 3 años), debe existir un Estatuto bajo las consideraciones del MEC.	Pueden sin dudas pero quienes se presenten deben registrarse y comprometerse a cumplir con los requerimientos de cualquier sociedad civil nacional	Hay que registrar esa organización en la Dirección Nacional de Registro, dependiente del Ministerio de Educación y Cultura. Cuando alguien decide abrir una ONG tiene que elegir entre dos figuras jurídicas : la fundación y la asociación civil sin fines de lucro	Entre 3 y 6 meses	No existen prohibiciones legales/administrativas. Debe presentarse con escribano público ante Ministerio de Educación y Cultura, con los libros (con un costo elevado) y que cuenta con un costo de más de mil de dólares sin incluir al Escribano.	Plena libertad de expresión	Una de las mayores preocupaciones que existen es la falta de fondos internacionales lo que lleva a la Sociedad Civil uruguaya a realizar convenios con organismos estatales y muchas veces se encuentran "atados" para no perder los fondos	Las ONGs en Uruguay se encuentran con exoneración fiscal, aquellas que cuenten con personal contratado o deben estar al día con el pago de los aportes al Banco de Previsión Social	El control lo realiza el propio Ministerio de Educación y Cultura. Se deben presentar informes anuales. El Poder Ejecutivo, a propuesta del Ministerio de Educación y Cultura, podrá disponer la intervención de las asociaciones civiles y fundaciones como medida cautelar:

VENEZUELA	Constitución de la Republica (1999), Código Civil y leyes fiscales	Se pueden Notariar los estatutos y documento constitutivo ante Notario Público y en años recientes también se requiere el registro ante una Oficina de Registro Subalterno. A pesar de ser un sistema simple de presentación de estatutos y documento el gobierno extraoficialmente impide el proceso de registro de organizaciones.	La Ley no establecía ninguna limitación y las organizaciones simplemente legalizaban y traducían sus documentos constitutivos y se presentaban ante la Oficina de Registro Subalterno. Ahora con la delegación al Gobierno Cubano de las oficinas de registro es prácticamente imposible registrar una organización extranjera en el país.	No existe sistema de Registro, sin embargo el Proyecto de Ley de Cooperación Internacional (aprobado en primera discusión en el Congreso) establece un Registro integral de organizaciones. De acuerdo con Redsoc existen 960 organizaciones registradas en Venezuela	Antes del Gobierno actual se registraban en dos semanas y si se "habilitaba" el registro en un lapso no mayor de 48 horas. Ahora el rango es entre 6 meses a 1 año cuando se logran registrar.	El gobierno persigue organizaciones de derechos humanos, democracia y de actividades que no estén en línea con la "revolución". En Diciembre de 2010 se aprobó la Ley de Protección de la Libertad Política y la Autodeterminación (Ley de Soberanía) que restringe y sanciona con multas y cierre a organizaciones que emitan opiniones o hagan actividades que puedan ser percibidas como críticas al gobierno.	La Ley de Soberanía persigue al financiamiento internacional restringiendo la operación y la opinión de personas y organizaciones. El Proyecto de Ley de Cooperación Internacional precisamente crea un Fondo concentrado que limita la libre obtención de recursos y además el gobierno persigue a organizaciones que reciben fondos internacionales. Hay además sentencias del Tribunal Supremo que persiguen a las organizaciones. La Ley de ilícitos cambiarios también persigue a las organizaciones que reciben fondos del extranjero.	El gobierno ha venido restringiendo la libertad de opinión e información, así como la libertad de internet y abiertamente persigue a las organizaciones, en foros internacionales como la OEA y la ONU restringe y evita la participación de organizaciones de Venezuela que le puedan ser críticas. Las leyes de Partidos Políticos y la "Ley de Soberanía" limitan más aun la libertad de opinión de organizaciones de la sociedad civil.	Hasta el año 2002 el Seniat otorgaba exoneración del Impuesto sobre la Renta a organizaciones sin fines de lucro sin mayores limitaciones mediante un proceso sencillo de envío de la solicitud. A partir de esa fecha la obtención de la exoneración es prácticamente imposible. De igual forma solo acceden a otorgarla a organizaciones con fines Culturales, Deportivas y Científicas.	No existen obligaciones formales de información, salvo el caso laboral o fiscal. El proyecto de Ley de Cooperación requiere de informes permanentes, informes al ser requeridos y un sistema integral de control. Hay la obligación de informar sobre los fondos en moneda extranjera recibidos. La disolución esta prevista en los estatutos de cada organización, sin embargo el Proyecto de Ley de Cooperación incluye esta facultad para el gobierno.

Argentina: Cesar Murua y Juan Carballo para el WMD y Marta Gaba para la RLCD
Bolivia: Informe elaborado por Ramiro Orias para el WMD
Brasil: Carlos Ponce con información del Ministerio de Justicia http://portal.mj.gov.br y de http://www.abong.org.br
Chile: Informe Elaborado por Maria Inés de Ferrari para el WMD
Colombia: Adriana Ruíz-Restrepo para el WMD
Costa Rica: Informe elaborado por Pablo Innecken para la RLCD
Cuba: Carlos E. Ponce, análisis de la Ley No. 54 y su reglamento
Ecuador: Dra. Blanca Gómez de la Torre para el WMD
El Salvador: Informe Elaborado por José Marinero Cortes para el World Movement for Democracy
Guatemala: Informe elaborado por el World Movement for Democracy
Honduras: Carlos E. Ponce
México: Informe presentado Cirila Quintero y Rommel González a la RLCD
Nicaragua: Defendiendo la Sociedad Civil, Reflexiones y Posicionamiento de Organizaciones de la Sociedad Civil, Varias Organizaciones, Julio 2009.
Nicaragua: Informe del NGO Law Monitor del International Center for Non for Profit Law
Panamá: Informe elaborado por Magaly Castillo para el WMD
Paraguay: Enrique Néstor Sosa A. para el WMD
Perú: Informe elaborado por el World Movement for Democracy
República Dominicana: Informe elaborado por Rommel Santos para la RLCD
Uruguay: Rosa Quintana para la Red Latinoamericana y del Caribe para la Democracia
Venezuela: Informe elaborado por Carlos E. Ponce

About the Author

Dr. Carlos Ponce is the general coordinator of the Latin American and Caribbean Network for Democracy, a network of over 300 leading civil society organizations across the Americas. He is expert on human rights, environmental justice, civil society, and democracy in Latin America and the Caribbean, he has been lecturer and professor at Tufts University, Venezuela's Central University, Thomas Moore Global University and AB Catholic University. He is a elected member of the steering committees of the World Movement for Democracy and the ISC Community of Democracies. In his native Venezuela, Dr. Ponce successfully founded and led the Justice and Development Consortium (Asociación Civil Consorcio Desarrollo y Justicia) a nongovernmental organization that develops justice-reform and conflict-resolution programs at the local level and advised several civil society organizations, including the student/youth movements in Venezuela and other countries of Latin America. He previously worked as executive secretary of Venezuela's National Human Rights Commission, as Professor at the Venezuela's Central University and as an advisor to the Venezuelan Congress. He gaduated from the AB catholic University (law), Tufts University (MA Urban and Environmental Policy and Planning), Vermont Law School (MS Environmental Law)(Magna Cum Laude), Northeastern University (Doctor in Law and Policy) and he is an alumnae from Fulbright, Department of State Visitor Program, European Union Visitor Program and Reagan-Fascell Democracy Fellowship.

---

i Declaration on the Right and Responsibility of Individuals, Groups and Organs of Society to Promote and Protect Universally Recognized Human Rights and Fundamental Freedoms, General Assembly resolution 53/144, G.A. res.53/144, annex, 53 UN GAOR Supp., UN Doc. UN Doc. A/RES/53/144 (1999), Article 18(3)

ii "Civil society" constitutes that element outside of government and business sectors, both organized and essentially disorganized, that represents the engagement of people among and with one another to achieve their aspirations, meet their needs, and live creative, active, healthy lives. To define the term much more precisely actually works to limit it, when in fact the essential characteristic of "civil society" is its unlimited quality. Douglas Rutzen and Catherine Shea, "The associational counter-revolution" (2006) Volume 11, Number 3. Alliance Magazine (www.alliancemagazine.org)

iii Elements of Freedom of Association: A. The Right to Establish an Association with Legal Personality. This includes the Right to Registration required in order for an NGO to attain legal personality; B. The Right to Join (Or Not to Join) an Organization; C. The Right to Request, Obtain and Manage Licit Financial Resources; D.

The Right to Affiliate with Other National and International Organizations; E. The Duty of the governments to avoid Unreasonable Interference in Internal Governance. Source: The Neglected Right: Freedom of Association in International Human Rights Law

iv In a report, developed by the World Movement for Democracy Steering Committee and the International Center for Not for Profit Law (ICNL) called "Defending Civil Society" we had the opportunity to open consultations for all the regions with meetings in several cities and we found troublesome similarities among different regimes that persecute or imposed limitations/restrictions to civil society. That report came after an intensive consultation process worldwide. According with the report, legal constrains against civil society fall broadly into five categories:

- Barriers to entry (limited right to associate, prohibition against unregistered groups, restrictions on founders, burdensome registration/incorporation procedures, vague grounds for denial, re-registration requirements, barriers for international organizations)
- Barriers for operational Activity (direct prohibitions against spheres of activity, invasive supervisory oversight, government harassment, criminal sanctions against individuals, failure to protect individuals, termination and dissolution, establishment of GONGOs)
- Barriers to Speech and Advocacy (prior restrains and censorship, defamation laws, vague restrictions against advocacy, criminalization of dissent, restrictions on freedom of assembly)
- Barriers to contact and Communication (barriers to the creation of networks, barriers to international contact, barriers to communication, criminal sanctions against individuals)
- Barriers to resources (Prohibition against funding, advance government approval, routing founding through the government).Barriers to contact and Communication (barriers to the creation of networks, barriers to international contact, barriers to communication, criminal sanctions against individuals)
- Barriers to resources (Prohibition against funding, advance government approval, routing founding through the government).

v In July 2006 the author had a meeting at the UN in New York with Viktor Yushchenko His government and the changes in Ukraine were a by-product of the "Orange Revolution", and when we asked him about support against Russia, Venezuela, Zimbabwe, Iran, Egypt and other countries with limitations or persecutions against civil society organizations or activist, he basically said that "sometimes limitations are useful because you cannot have so powerful groups controlling each activity of the governments". More dramatic examples of reverse feelings toward NGOs and civil society, after successful civil society revolutions, can be seen in Russia and more recently in Georgia.

vi Adong, Florence, Rising from the Ashes: The Rebirth of Civil Society in Authoritarian Political Environment, *The International Journal of Not-for-Profit Law*, Volume 10, Issue 3, (June 2008).

vii US Department of State, Supra Note 89

viii Closing statement of Human Rights First to the Working Group on Human Rights Defenders–March 4, 1998

ix International Center for Not-for-Profit Law (INCL), "Recent Laws and Legislative Proposals to Restrict Civil Society and Civil Society Organizations" (2006) Volume 8, Issue 4. The International Journal of Not-for-Profit Law.

x The Human Rights Committee must be distinguished from the Commission on Human Rights, a Charter-based mechanism, and its replacement, the Human Rights Council. In contrast to the Commission on Human Rights, a political forum where states debated all human rights concerns (replaced by the Council in 2006), the Human Rights Committee is a treaty-based mechanism pertaining only to the International Covenant on Civil and Political Rights.

xi David Moore, "Safeguarding Civil Society in Politically Complex Environments" (2007) Volume 9, Issue 3. The International Journal of Not-for-Profit Law. [Moore] ; see the Human Rights Committee, http://www.frontlinedefenders.org/manual/en/hrc_m.htm.

xii See the Human Rights Committee, http://www.frontlinedefenders.org/manual/en/hrc_m.htm. See also Office of the United Nations High Commissioner for Human Rights, http://www.ohchr.org/english/issues/defenders/index.htm.

xiii See the Human Rights Committee, http://www.frontlinedefenders.org/manual/en/hrc_m.htm.

xiv International Center for Not-for-Profit Law (INCL), "Recent Laws and Legislative Proposals to Restrict Civil Society and Civil Society Organizations" (2006) Volume 8, Issue 4. The International Journal of Not-for-Profit Law.

xv Moore, supra note 97; See Promoting Justice, pp. 65-66.

xvi The International Center for Not-for-Profit Law, International Investment Treaty Protection of Not-for-Profit Organizations, June 2007, Regional NGO Law Rapid-Response Mechanism, Supported by USAID

xvii The International Center for Not-for-Profit Law, International Investment Treaty Protection of Not-for-Profit Organizations, June 2007, Regional NGO Law Rapid-Response Mechanism, Supported by USAID

xviii International Center for Not-for-Profit Law (INCL), "Recent Laws and Legislative Proposals to Restrict Civil Society and Civil Society Organizations" (2006) Volume 8, Issue 4. The International Journal of Not-for-Profit Law.

xix KC, Rajendra. 2003. NGO's Development and Management: NGOs' Illusion and Reality, Kathmandu: REDA

xx International Center for Not-for-Profit Law (INCL), "Recent Laws and Legislative Proposals to Restrict Civil Society and Civil Society Organizations" (2006) Volume 8, Issue 4. The International Journal of Not-for-Profit Law.

xxi International Center for Not-for-Profit Law (INCL), "Recent Laws and Legislative Proposals to Restrict Civil Society and Civil Society Organizations" (2006) Volume 8, Issue 4. The International Journal of Not-for-Profit Law.

xxii International Center for Not-for-Profit Law (INCL), "Recent Laws and Legislative Proposals to Restrict Civil Society and Civil Society Organizations" (2006) Volume 8, Issue 4. The International Journal of Not-for-Profit Law.

xxiii Moore, supra note 97; Chilean students end mass protest, News Limited, June 10, 2006.

xxiv International Center for Not-for-Profit Law (INCL), "Recent Laws and Legislative Proposals to Restrict Civil Society and Civil Society Organizations" (2006) Volume 8, Issue 4. The International Journal of Not-for-Profit Law.

xxv International Center for Not-for-Profit Law (INCL), "Recent Laws and Legislative Proposals to Restrict Civil Society and Civil Society Organizations" (2006) Volume 8, Issue 4. The International Journal of Not-for-Profit Law.

xxvi On August 2006, CIVICUS expresses concern that Venezuela 's proposed "International. CIVICUS called on the government of Venezuela to: a. Withdraw the bill in its current form and, through a consultative process, engage with Venezuelan civil society organizations on appropriate revisions. b. Abide by your commitments to uphold and protect freedom of association, as recognized under Venezuela's Constitution (Article 52); the American Convention on Human Rights (Article 16); and the International Covenant on Civil and Political Rights (Article 22).

xxvii "Recent Laws", supra note 9.

xxviii Moore, supra note 97

xxix See www.ngolaw.org.

xxx See http://www.civicus.org/csw/news.asp?section=updates&title=news.asp.

xxxi Campaigning for Freedom of Expression: A Handbook for Advocates, International Freedom of Expression Exchange (IFEX), p. 19.

xxxii David Moore, "Safeguarding Civil Society in Politically Complex Environments" (2007) Volume 9, Issue 3. The International Journal of Not-for-Profit Law.

xxxiii See http://www.freedomhouse.org; http://www.transparency.org; http://www.rsf.org; http://www.usaid.gov/locations/europe_eurasia/dem_gov/ngoindex; http://hrw.org/english/docs/2006/06/28/global14096.htm (June 29, 2006).

xxxiv Moore, supra note 97;

xxxv Moore, supra note 97;

xxxvi Moore, supra note 97

xxxvii Campaigning for Freedom of Expression: A Handbook for Advocates, International Freedom of Expression Exchange (IFEX), pp. 19-23.

xxxviii David Moore, "Safeguarding Civil Society in Politically Complex Environments" (2007) Volume 9, Issue 3. The International Journal of Not-for-Profit Law. [Moore]

xxxix Stephan E. Klingelhofer, and David Robinson, "Law and Civil Society in the South Pacific: Challenges and Opportunities; International Best Practices; and Global Developments" The International Center for Not-for-Profit Law (ICNL). 2004 --> Pages 4-16 set out a fairly detailed discussion the elements that the legal framework governing Civil Society should cover: the way an organization comes into existence, the regulation of their existence, and particular activities of these organizations. The article also discusses to what extent these aspects should be governed (if at all).

xl In order to be accountable to the society, the NGOs should take the questions raised by the society seriously, and do its own evaluation in a regular basis. Unless the issues of transparency and accountability are implemented sternly in the NGOs, the social prestige of the NGOs cannot be elevated.

xli This practice started with the signing of a Compact in England and the rest of the UK in 1998, and has continued with the signing of the Voluntary Sector Accord in Canada in 2001, and similar agreements in Eastern Europe.

xlii Adong, Florence, Rising from the Ashes: The Rebirth of Civil Society in Authoritarian Political Environment, The International Journal of Not-for-Profit Law, Volume 10, Issue 3, June 2008.

www.ingramcontent.com/pod-product-compliance
Lightning Source LLC
Chambersburg PA
CBHW060202290526
45789CB00003B/1126